SECTION E

Applying Group Work in the Community and in Schools

Other Books in the Group Work Practice Kit

Groups in Community and Agency Settings

Groups in Community and Agency Settings

Niloufer M. Merchant
St. Cloud State University

Carole J. Yozamp
St. Cloud Hospital

Los Angeles | London | New Delhi
Singapore | Washington DC

Los Angeles | London | New Delhi
Singapore | Washington DC

FOR INFORMATION:

SAGE Publications, Inc.
2455 Teller Road
Thousand Oaks, California 91320
E-mail: order@sagepub.com

SAGE Publications Ltd.
1 Oliver's Yard
55 City Road
London EC1Y 1SP
United Kingdom

SAGE Publications India Pvt. Ltd.
B 1/I 1 Mohan Cooperative Industrial Area
Mathura Road, New Delhi 110 044
India

SAGE Publications Asia-Pacific Pte. Ltd.
3 Church Street
#10-04 Samsung Hub
Singapore 049483

Acquisitions Editor: Kassie Graves
Editorial Assistant: Elizabeth Luizzi
Production Editor: Brittany Bauhaus
Copy Editor: Megan Granger
Typesetter: C&M Digitals (P) Ltd.
Proofreader: Rae-Ann Goodwin
Indexer: Marilyn Augst
Cover Designer: Anupama Krishnan
Marketing Manager: Shari Countryman

Copyright © 2014 by SAGE Publications, Inc.

Printed in the United States of America

Library of Congress Cataloging-in-Publication Data

A catalog record of this book is available from the Library of Congress.

9781483332246

This book is printed on acid-free paper.

Certified Chain of Custody
Promoting Sustainable Forestry
www.sfiprogram.org
SFI-01268

SFI label applies to text stock

13 14 15 16 17 10 9 8 7 6 5 4 3 2 1

Brief Contents _____

_____ Detailed Contents

Acknowledgments_____

W e would like to thank Katie Gunderson-Eccleston for assisting us with the many detailed tasks for the book. We thank our families, who were patient and supportive during the writing of this book. Most important, we thank Bob Conyne for the opportunity to share our experience and passion related to group work.

1   Introduction

Group work is offered in many different types of settings, with diverse populations, and with people who experience a wide range of problems. While the use of group work has been in existence for a number of years (Gladding, 2011), it has grown considerably in popularity over the past few decades (DeLucia-Waack, Gerrity, Kalodner, & Riva, 2004). Many factors have contributed to the widespread use of groups, including the ability to work with several people simultaneously, cost-effectiveness, and, most important, the benefit derived from the powerful group dynamics and interpersonal relationships (Yalom, 2005).

In this book, we've provided an overview of groups found in the community and a range of community agency settings along the continuum of prevention, intervention, and post-intervention. The chapters provide a description of the three main types of groups that fit along the continuum of care: (1) prevention groups, (2) groups in remedial treatment settings, and (3) support and self-help groups. The difference between these three types of groups can sometimes be blurred, depending on the type of setting and the approach used by group facilitators or members. We've attempted to tease out some of the differences, although it is evident that some of the distinctions made in theory are not always reflected in practice. We experienced this same tension as we were writing the book, as we bring different experiences to the table. I (Merchant) have an academic background with ongoing experience in the field, while I (Yozamp) have primarily a practitioner perspective. The practice of group work is much more ambiguous, with the terms *prevention, support,* and *counseling* or *therapy groups* sometimes used interchangeably. These dilemmas also raise an issue related to the gap between research and practice, and how this translates into best practices or evidence-based practice.

Nonetheless, in defining the types of groups, we have used the framework provided by the Association for Specialists in Group Work (ASGW) professional training standards (Wilson, Rapin, & Haley-Banez, 2000). ASGW defines the specialization of training in group work as including knowledge, skills, and experiences deemed necessary for counselors to engage in independent practice of group work. Four areas of advanced practice, referred to as specializations, are identified as task group facilitation, group psychoeducation, group counseling, and group psychotherapy. This list is not presumed to be exhaustive, and while there may be no sharp boundaries between the specializations, each has recognizable characteristics that have professional utility. Specialized training presumes mastery of prerequisite core knowledge, skills, and experiences. Key elements of these definitions are that group work is a broad professional practice oriented to help-giving or task accomplishment. That is, group work is comprehensive, not restricted to any one particular methodology, such as group counseling or group therapy. Moreover, group work can be used to help people grow and change—goals that are well within the heritage of group counseling—and to help people solve tasks and work problems. These concepts give rise to the evolution under way to make group work training more consistent with the growing intensity and diversity of demands for group work practice (Conyne, 2000).

In addition to utilizing the ASGW training standards (Wilson et al., 2000), we've also applied the principles of the ASGW *Best Practice Guidelines* (Thomas & Pender, 2008) and *Multicultural and Social Justice Competence Principles* (Singh, Merchant, Skudrzyk, & Ingene, 2012) to the context of prevention groups, groups in remedial settings, and support and self-help groups. We've described in detail the three Ps of best practice—planning, performing, and processing—and addressed multicultural and social justice principles for each of the steps in the process. At the end of each chapter, we have provided specific examples that demonstrate how groups are implemented in the various contexts.

The chapter on prevention groups provides an overview of the role of prevention groups in the community. We address the use of psychoeducational groups in prevention and provide a step-by-step process on how to plan for and implement such groups using the *Best Practice Guidelines* and *Multicultural and Social Justice Competence Principles*, as defined by ASGW.

The third chapter focuses on the various types of groups in remedial treatment centers, ranging from health care settings, private practice, inpatient and outpatient treatment, and residential treatment centers. As noted in the chapter, there is a role in remediation for all four types of groups—task, psychoeducational, counseling, and psychotherapy. Examples of evidence-based treatment practices—such as trauma-focused cognitive behavioral therapy, as implemented in a residential treatment setting for children and adolescents—are discussed. An additional example of a psychoeducation group in an outpatient setting for children and adolescents is also provided.

The last chapter addresses self-help or mutual aid and support groups in community settings. The growth of self-help and support groups in recent years has been a force to reckon with; helping professionals, while initially reluctant, are now accepting the role of such groups as an adjunct or sometimes even the sole form of treatment delivery. In the chapter on support and self-help groups, we explore the differences as well as the blurring of these groups. Concrete examples are provided on how to develop and conduct support groups using the ASGW best practices and multicultural principles, with two very different illustrations of such a group.

Needless to say, this book covers a wide range of group work practice in community settings. We hope you will find this book useful in understanding the different types of group offered, along with the hands-on tips of how best to implement such groups.

2   Prevention Groups

The call bell for prevention groups has long been sounded by many leading professionals (Conyne, 2000, 2010; Hage & Romano, 2010; Owens & Kulic, 2001; Romano & Hage, 2000), as well as professional organizations such as the American Psychological Association (APA; see Conyne, 2010), Counseling Psychology (Division 17 of APA), and the Society for Prevention Research. The science and practice of prevention is deemed essential to prevent many physical, mental, and social problems. According to the *Call for Bold Action to Support Prevention Programs and Policies* (Society for Prevention Research, 2009), prevention science findings are clear. In this document, the task force affirms that "carefully implemented, certain tested and effective or 'evidence-based' programs and policies clearly prevent a wide range of problems among youth and families, promote positive youth development, and simultaneously achieve economic benefits" (p. 1).

Despite these calls for action, the movement toward implementation has been slow. One of the reasons cited for this sluggish progress has been not only lack of guidance and training on how to conduct prevention groups but also lack of information on what prevention is and how it works (Conyne, 1991, 2010). Prevention, which has its roots in public health (Owens & Kulic, 2001), is considered tangential to the practice of counseling and psychology, with primary emphasis given to remedial efforts (Romano & Hage, 2000). As much as prevention is seen as desirable by most mental health practitioners, lack of funding (Hage & Romano, 2010) and prioritization of prevention programs by agencies and institutions makes it all the harder to implement such programs. Insurance companies and other third-party payers reimburse only for treatment of specified disorders. Limited options are available for funding prevention programs or groups, and those options sometimes require navigating through cumbersome processes and procedures. This has often been the case in our experience. First, there is a fair amount of preplanning that entails convincing agency directors, school principals, or program directors of the benefits of offering prevention programs within their settings. This is often followed by writing grants or pursuing other creative means to explore funding options. Funding for prevention programs tends to come from "soft" money through grants or other temporary allocations. The current downturn in the economy has put funding for prevention programs in further jeopardy. A recent column in *Politico* (Smith, 2012) reports that federal funding for various prevention programs, such as tobacco and suicide prevention, and community grants for the promotion of healthy lifestyles and other health-related issues are in jeopardy. Another barrier faced by counseling and psychology professionals is whether providing prevention services is considered part of their job duties. If offering prevention services is not part of one's regular job, then doing so requires going above and beyond one's normal responsibilities. These challenges can sometimes seem daunting and can effectively discourage the implementation of prevention programs.

To lower these barriers, Conyne (2000) proposed a "Resolution" for the counseling psychology field to provide more attention to prevention through increased training, research, practice, and advocacy. The APA has promoted and sponsored prevention programs through such efforts as the Psychologically Healthy Workplace Awards; Practice, Science and Public Interest Directories; Violence Prevention Office; and the Prevention Section of Division 17, Counseling Psychology (see Conyne, 2010). Similarly, the Association for Specialists in Group Work (ASGW), in their revised *Professional Standards for the Training of Group Workers* (Wilson, Rapin, & Haley-Banez, 2000) expanded the understanding of groups to include prevention as one of the major purposes underlying group practice. One area of prevention that has received considerable attention is on university and college campuses. Romano and Hage (2000) report an increased and sustained focus on the part of higher educational systems over the past few decades to provide prevention offerings on such topics as stress management, drug and alcohol use, and wellness. In the past decade, the issue of bullying prevention has gained considerable attention, with many K–12 schools incorporating specific curricula in classroom settings. Recognition and resources provided by professional associations and educational institutions, as well as the recent advances in positive psychology and the role of positive emotions (Fredrickson, 2009) and mindfulness practices such as mindfulness-based stress reduction (Kabat-Zinn, 1990) and mindfulness-based relapse prevention (Bowen, Chawla, & Marlatt, 2011) have generated renewed excitement and interest in prevention strategies and groups.

What Are Prevention Groups? _____

Prevention groups are designed to reduce the incidence of future harm and facilitate health-promoting and risk-reducing behaviors. The populations most often targeted for prevention are those groups of people who are presently healthy and/or considered to be at risk for disturbance (Owens & Kulic, 2001). Prevention efforts have been categorized by three levels of intervention: primary (decrease the incidence of a disorder), secondary (reduce the prevalence by targeting populations at risk), and tertiary (decrease the negative effects of an existing disorder). There is some debate regarding whether secondary and tertiary prevention are, in fact, remediation rather than differing levels of prevention (Romano & Hage, 2000). The complex nature of prevention makes it difficult at times to discern between the three levels, but one thing they all have in common is the reduction of future risk or harm. Romano and Hage have expanded the definition of prevention from one of simply reducing incidence, onset, and impact of problem behaviors to one that includes interventions that enhance personal well-being, as well as supporting institutional policies that promote physical and emotional well-being.

The promotion of prevention through group work has long been documented (see Hage & Romano, 2010) and considered to be a natural fit for mental health prevention goals (Conyne, 2004). A comprehensive definition provided by Conyne and Wilson (2000) states that groups for prevention are those that

> involve small numbers of members who are generally healthy or are at risk for the development of an identified physical or psychosocial dysfunction and who meet face-to-face with a trained group leader(s). Members interact with each other focusing on an appropriate blend of content (e.g., social skills development; psychoactive substance use and abuse information) and process (e.g., cognitive clarification, interpersonal feedback, consciousness raising, group decision making) consistent with the focus and structure of the group. The general purpose is to gain knowledge and skills that will empower them to avoid future harmful events and situations and to live their lives more meaningfully and productively. (p. 10)

As noted in the definition, the combination of content or educational factors, along with process (which includes interaction between members and other group dynamic issues), allows for conditions to promote knowledge, growth, and healing. According to Conyne (2004), the group format is preferred in offering preventive interventions, as groups are cost-effective, therapeutically efficacious, and provide a venue to impact a number of people at the same time (a particularly relevant goal of prevention), within the context of social support.

While most types of groups can be used for prevention services, psychoeducational groups are purported to be most suited for prevention purposes (Conyne, 2004; Conyne & Horne, 2001; Owens & Kulic, 2001) and are identified as one of eight domains necessary to promote the advancement of prevention training, practice, and research (Romano & Hage, 2000).

Psychoeducational Groups in Prevention

ASGW identifies four types of groups in its standards for training group workers (Wilson et al., 2000): (1) task or work groups (for the accomplishment of specific tasks), (2) psychoeducational groups (for promoting education, development, and growth), (3) counseling groups (for promoting personal and interpersonal growth), and (4) therapy groups (for remedial purposes with those who have severe and chronic maladjustment). Of these four types of groups, the psychoeducational format is considered to provide the best forum to transmit information, build skills, and assist members in coping with their daily lives. Membership in these groups typically entails those people who may be healthy or at risk and not experiencing significant dysfunction in the area of focus (Owens & Kulic, 2001). According to Conyne (2004), psychoeducational groups include several factors that are central to prevention, such as setting specific goals; providing structured, time-limited experiences; focusing on skill development; emphasizing application to real life; and processing group interactions and other psychological processes in the here-and-now context.

Therapeutic Factors in Prevention Groups

While psychoeducational groups may be the best fit for prevention groups, other formats for offering prevention groups also need to be explored. For instance, prevention groups are offered in health care settings as a way to prevent more serious medical concerns. An example of such a group would be a group for individuals who are pre-diabetic or may be prone to heart disease as a result of being overweight. Healthy eating, nutritional tips, exercising, and ways to prepare a healthy meal may be some of the topics explored in this prevention group. Because of the heavy content focus in this group, it would be very easy for a leader who is not trained in group interaction to make the mistake of focusing only on content and ignoring the underlying process. Harpine, Nitza, and Conyne (2010), however, argue that group process is equally important to address in prevention groups. The 11 therapeutic factors proposed by Yalom (2005)—instillation of hope, universality, imparting information, altruism, recapitulation of the primary family group, development of socializing techniques, imitative behaviors, interpersonal learning, group cohesiveness, catharsis, and existential factors—are considered to be important process dynamics that emerge in the cycle of the group. While these therapeutic factors were identified primarily in the context of counseling and therapy groups, they may also play a significant role in prevention groups.

For group prevention to be successful, Harpine et al. (2010) emphasize the need to pay attention to "the power of group process, interaction between group members, and the warmth of group cohesion" (p. 269). When consideration is given to group process in prevention groups, the therapeutic factors suggested by Yalom (2005) can become especially meaningful. For instance, the overarching themes of *hope* and *universality* are embedded in the basic conceptualization of prevention groups. Hope is evident in the belief that change is possible and we can improve our lives. The aspect of *universality* is apparent as prevention groups bring together people with a shared focal problem as a way to help them see that they are not alone in experiencing that problem. Furthermore, prevention groups depend on *imparting information,* with greater benefits received from this therapeutic factor when group members are more active rather than passive in their learning process. As group members interact with one another, they learn the power of *altruism* and an increased sense of satisfaction in helping others. *Interpersonal learning, imitative learning,* and the *development of social skills* also occur as group members learn and practice new skills within the group. While catharsis and family reenactment may occur to a lesser degree, group facilitators need to be watchful of these factors as they emerge and need to have the necessary skills to help create meaning of group members' thoughts and feelings. Over the years, we have observed that group facilitators who are not trained in group interaction are uncomfortable acknowledging the underlying emotions and process issues, resulting in issues being avoided or the group focus being derailed. Also, appropriate referrals to other helping sources may be needed for members who require more intervention than can be provided in a prevention group. Finally, attention to meaningful interactions among group members is likely to lead to *group cohesion* and a sense of belonging, which in turn serves as a catalyst for change (Harpine et al., 2010).

Best Practices in Leading Prevention Groups

Best practices delineated by ASGW (Thomas & Pender, 2008) offer guidelines and a conceptual framework for the implementation of effective groups. These best practice guidelines include the following three functions that group workers are responsible for: (1) planning—the logistical tasks of assessing need, identifying group goals, setting group structure, determining resources, screening members, selecting facilitators, and the like; (2) performing—the adaptive implementation of the plan, generating meaning, and creating the therapeutic conditions necessary to maximize group experience; and (3) processing—the reflective practice of processing group workings with members, supervisors, and colleagues, as well as evaluating process and outcome of the group. A more recent ASGW document on *Multicultural and Social Justice Competence Principles for Group Workers* (Singh, Merchant, Skudrzyk, & Ingene, 2012) provides guidelines on the integration of multicultural and social justice issues for each of these functions. Conyne (2004) incorporated the best practice principles in identifying several steps in implementing prevention groups. The following steps are adapted from Conyne's recommendations for prevention groups and integrated with the current multicultural and social justice competence principles.

Planning

1. The first step is to identify the target population and their needs through an ecological assessment, which takes into consideration the needs, values, and culture of prospective members (Conyne & Bemak, 2004). The assessment can be conducted through interviews, surveys, and focus groups. An assessment of the culture of the population and issues related to class, gender, race and ethnicity, sexual orientation, age, disability, and immigration status should be taken into consideration. It is important to exhibit an understanding of how these factors are likely to intersect with help-seeking behaviors, the type of issues faced, and the manner in which these issues can be resolved. The overall group focus and content should fit the needs and context of the target population.

2. Partnering with the target population in developing the goals and design of the group is the next critical step, as oftentimes the target population is not engaged in the planning, which creates a sense of being "done to" rather than being "part of" the process. Partnering with the target population helps build collaboration and investment into the process, as well as a way to demonstrate respect. This is an important step in any circumstance but is even more critical when entering a cultural context different from one's own. It is also important to seek understanding of the cultural heritage, life experiences, and worldviews of members of the population and incorporate their perspectives in designing the group. Basic issues such as location, time, provision of transportation, child care, food, and so forth can be determined much more easily by partnering with the population. Community "elders," leaders, or experts should be consulted as appropriate in designing the group. Attention also needs to be given to language needs and ways they will be addressed—for example, identifying facilitators that speak the language, determining use of interpreters, and disseminating materials in appropriate languages.

3. Identifying a body of literature that is pertinent to the focal area and the type of population served is also important. Collecting information on best practices for the type of group being developed, connecting with local agencies that provide similar resources, and gathering updated resources and materials relevant to the focus of the group help ensure quality and relevance of the group. Prevention group leaders must also seek to understand the population being served and the impact of multicultural issues relevant to perception of time, styles of communication, cultural history, and background.

4. The goals, structure, and evaluation plan should then be determined collaboratively with the target population. The establishing of

group goals and structure should take into consideration the focus of the group, the type of outcome desired, and the nature of the population being served. Depending on the multicultural context of the population served, groups may be structured in a way that best addresses the diversity needs of the group. Merchant (2006, 2009) has identified three types of diversity-related groups: (1) culture-specific groups (people who share a common experience as a result of their diversity), (2) intercultural learning groups (designed to promote cultural understanding across groups), and (3) other-content–focused groups (focused on other issues but consider diversity issues within the group). Therefore, an HIV prevention group offered in a community center located within a predominantly Latino community may specifically target Latino males. Furthermore, goals of the group may involve prevention of a problem (in this case, prevention of HIV), promotion of healthy or safe practices (e.g., safe sex, use of sterile intravenous needles), or both. Finally, planning an evaluation component in advance is crucial to the success of the group. According to Conyne (2003), evaluation is a key step that distinguishes prevention groups from other programs, but it is often overlooked.

5. A detailed plan that delineates goals, recruitment, leader qualifications and responsibilities, screening, membership, group setting, session-by-session activities, information and strategies, group developmental model, and evaluation should be created. Since prevention groups generally follow a psychoeducational model, the plan can be specific and detailed. Modifications can be made along the way as needed; however, having a plan in place allows for smoother implementation, delivery, and evaluation. Group goals should be concise and focused, with an emphasis toward goal accomplishment. Activities planned need to be culturally grounded and relevant to the target population.

6. Leader(s) selected for the group should match the needs of the group and group goals. Cultural context and language needs of the group should be taken into consideration; leaders immersed in a particular cultural context and/or having the ability to communicate in the languages spoken by the members are likely to be seen as more credible and trustworthy. The use of interpreters may need to be addressed; however, it is important to exercise caution, as interpretation in a group context can be complex and cumbersome.

7. As appropriate, members need to be screened for inclusion in the prevention group. Prevention groups are often geared toward populations that have homogeneity in the problem area (e.g., assisting immigrant populations with adjusting to the host culture); however, heterogeneity in other factors can be intentional. Composition or

balance of gender, age, educational background, socioeconomic status, and other social statuses, in addition to the type of diversity-related group, should be determined, as discussed earlier. Attention needs to be given to issues related to isolation of a group member as a result of being the "only one" who is different from the group. Use screening mechanisms that are culturally appropriate, making sure written materials explain rules, contract, and the like, and are in the preferred language of the member(s). Prevention groups are generally targeted toward a certain population, with an eye toward goal accomplishment, and, hence, brevity is encouraged (Conyne, 2003).

Performing

1. Prevention groups require a careful balance of information delivery, skill development, and attention to group process. While at times leader-to-member style may be appropriate in delivering information, it is equally important to promote growth and learning through member-to-member interaction and group processes.

2. Group norms established early on should create respect and valuing of one another. It is important to create an atmosphere that encourages open dialogue on differences in values, perspectives, and culture, at the same time working toward building cohesion. Intragroup differences need to be attended to, particularly as they relate to communication styles, gender, age, sexual orientation, disability, culture/race/ethnicity, and other social statuses.

3. Techniques used for skill development need to match the needs, values, and cultural context of the target population. Conyne and Wilson (1999) suggest using a performance model that sequences skill development in the following manner: Present content, describe relevant skill, demonstrate the skill, practice with each other, give performance feedback, discuss application to real world, retry the skill, and, finally, discuss and process as a large group.

4. Social justice advocacy is especially relevant for prevention groups, in that prevention efforts are usually aimed at improving conditions and enhancing wellness in the community at large. This often entails group leaders taking the extra steps of serving as advocates or allies, understanding how current policies, procedures, and laws prevent access to resources, and addressing change at a systemic level by exercising institutional intervention skills (Singh et al., 2012). Advocacy can take the form of promoting access to the group itself by addressing external needs such as transportation, child care, provision of food, and the like, or it can be on a larger scale of lobbying for change at the institutional or legislative level.

Processing

1. Processing group dynamics with group members and amongst leaders between group sessions is an important aspect of the learning process. Meaning attribution and connection of here-and-now behaviors with real-life circumstances enhances learning and promotes growth among members (Yalom, 2005). Similarly, leaders need to allow time between groups to process their experiences with one another and/or with supervisors or other consultants.

2. Evaluation of the process and outcome of groups is of the utmost importance in demonstrating effectiveness. Prevention groups in particular have been criticized for insufficient evaluative data (Conyne, 2003). Both formative and summative measures are recommended to conduct a comprehensive evaluation. Additionally, assessments used should be culturally appropriate, with careful consideration of impact on the community. Marginalized groups have often been exploited or overanalyzed, and, hence, evaluation measures should be used with sensitivity and in a way that will benefit and empower the community.

Example of a Prevention-Based Psychoeducational Group

As discussed in previous sections, the psychoeducational format provides an ideal forum for prevention groups. I (Merchant) have conducted several psychoeducational groups with children and adolescents of color to enhance cultural knowledge, cultural identity, and self-empowerment. These groups were offered in a variety of settings, including a long-term residential treatment setting for troubled youth, after-school programs for children in elementary school (kindergarten through third grade, and fourth through sixth grade), and girls in regular and alternative high schools. The original impetus for the group came from the need to provide a supportive environment for children and youth of color within various predominantly White educational and treatment settings. The overall purpose of the groups was to develop positive cultural identity through cultural awareness and activism. Specifically, the goals included enhancement of self-esteem by strengthening cultural and racial identity, increasing positive adjustment by becoming more aware of one's own and others' cultural backgrounds, and learning coping and survival skills to function in a predominantly White environment, which was sometimes perceived as hostile and unsupportive. The group served the preventive goals of strengthening knowledge, attitudes, and behaviors that promote personal well-being, as proposed by Romano and Hage (2000), within a culturally specific group environment that provided a sense of safety and support (Merchant, 2006). I will elaborate further on features, format, and activities for the groups for girls of color in a high school setting as one example of a psychoeducational prevention group.

Planning

Identifying Need and Partnering With Target Population

The local school district had identified a major gap in educational achievement of students of color compared with their White counterparts. I (Merchant) had served as an interim diversity co-coordinator for 1 year and had found that the schools lacked adequate support systems for students of color, particularly related to responding to the specific needs of students who came from lower-income backgrounds, coupled with their experience of prejudice and racism in the schools. Furthermore, school counselors were overwhelmed with their high case loads and could not devote the time needed to address the issues students of color were facing on a day-to-day basis. As a result of a partnership between the university, school district, and local sexual assault center, psychoeducational groups for girls of color who were struggling socially, emotionally, and academically were established in two high schools and one alternative learning center for youth. Groups were needed for girls and boys; however, due to the involvement of the sexual assault center, whose efforts were primarily focused on prevention efforts for girls, and my own interest in working with girls and women, it was decided to offer a girls group, with other efforts needed for boys of color. Much time and effort was spent in preplanning with the various stakeholders, as we had to navigate the bureaucracy of the various school systems; get buy-in from the counselors, social workers, and school principals; and obtain sufficient funding to conduct these groups. The local sexual assault center was a key partner in the collaboration, as it assigned some of its staff working on prevention efforts in K–12 schools to cofacilitate the groups in the high schools.

Group Structure

Each of the groups comprised five to eight ethnic-minority girls aged 14 to 18. As part of the screening process, referrals were sought from school counselors, vice principals, and teachers. The facilitators met with each of the girls to gauge interest and fit, and to explain the purpose of the group. The groups were conducted weekly by a school counselor and me (Merchant) for some of the groups, or with a staff member from the local sexual assault center. The groups met for about 8 weeks for one class period during the school day, and group times were rotated each week so that students didn't miss the same class repeatedly.

Performing and Processing

Group Norms and Rules

The first two sessions focused on establishing group norms and rules, and identifying topic areas of interest to the group members. In general, the girls were excited to have this opportunity to work with one another and were eager to cooperate. There were some instances where a few of the girls had prior conflict or unresolved issues with other group members. These issues were dealt with as they arose in the group and resulted in conflict resolution, identified as one of the focal areas for the group. Norms were developed to value individual and cultural differences, to maintain confidentiality, and to have a basic respect for one another. Emphasis was placed on creating a safe space for honest and open interactions.

Group Format and Activities

The groups followed a semistructured format to allow for processing of emerging issues within both the school and the group. The groups focused on the goal of enhancing gender and cultural/racial identity, and promoting a more positive adjustment in their school and home environments. Activities included discussion, watching excerpts of videos, role play, arts and crafts, and other experiential activities. Group dynamics and member interactions were addressed in the "here and now," giving them an opportunity to practice concepts and skills learned. Sample topics included the following:

- *Body image/beauty*—as defined in society and how they view themselves
- *Sexuality*—discussion on teen sex, dating, use of sex to define identity, and sexual violence
- *Healthy relationships*—differentiating between healthy and unhealthy relationships
- *Cultural identity*—discussion of their own cultural and racial identity development, learning more about their own and other members' cultural and racial heritage
- *Understanding and coping with racism*—learning about different forms of racism, discussing how they were personally impacted by racism, and considering ways they could address racism at a personal and institutional level
- *Inter- and intraethnic conflict and conflict resolution*—addressing conflicts among members and conflicts outside of the group, identifying appropriate conflict-resolution methods, and examining inter- and intraethnic conflicts

Group Evaluation

No formal evaluation was conducted; however, informal feedback from members (during the final sessions and in follow-up interviews with facilitators and counselors) indicated that the focused time spent with other girls of color and with the female facilitators, some of whom were women of color, were meaningful. Group members also reported that information learned from the groups helped them develop a more positive identity—both personally and culturally. The information gathered from these groups eventually led to a more elaborate 5-year grant project that prepared women university students to become mentors to girls of color in the high schools (Subrahmanyan & Merchant, 2006). Mentoring activities included one-on-one interactions as well as groups with girls of color in the junior high and high schools. The overarching goal of the project was to create an intergenerational network for women and girls—junior high and high school girls of color, women university students, and other adults in the university, school, and community. The idea behind the project was that girls needed emotional, social, *and* academic support to succeed in the school system, which could be accomplished through more focused one-on-one and small-group interactions.

Our biggest challenge in conducting these groups was to sustain them. As identified earlier, "soft" funding (through grants or temporary funding) devoted to such prevention efforts maintains these endeavors only as far as the funding and support remain. Sometimes efforts are tied to individual rather than systemic efforts; therefore, change in personnel in the various agencies can result in the death of these projects. Although we (Subrahmanyan and Merchant) are no longer involved in these services, we were able to ensure sustenance of the program through a university-based program that provides outreach to culturally diverse youth, particularly in relation to academic support. Therefore, the program we initiated for 8 years has now expanded to boys and girls from culturally diverse backgrounds and continues to be offered in the local public schools through one-on-one mentoring efforts. The focus has shifted more to academic support, but some of the fundamental concepts of provision of emotional and social support have been maintained.

Conclusion

The need for more prevention programs and groups continues to be reinforced as we continue to see sky-rocketing health care costs. Many urgent calls have been made to the counseling and psychology field by leading professionals, resulting in some gains in the field through such efforts as the establishment of best practice prevention guidelines for psychologists and the endorsement of prevention programs in health care reform (Hage & Romano, 2010). Owens and Kulic (2001) forecast that "increasing pressures will emerge for counselors to help people stay well through service delivery modes that are anticipatory, briefer, economical, and effective" (p. 208). As such, helping professions have an obligation to focus more efforts in the training, practice, and research of prevention groups. The ASGW *Best Practice Guidelines* (Thomas & Pender, 2008) and *Multicultural and Social Justice Competence Principles* (Singh et al., 2012) provide important guidelines in the appropriate planning, performing, and processing of various types of groups, and can be effectively applied to prevention groups. The psychoeducational group format is found to provide the best fit for prevention groups; therefore, knowledge and training in facilitating such groups would be most beneficial in the provision of prevention services. Needless to say, the more attention we give to offering prevention groups and prevention efforts in general, the more likely we will improve the overall wellness and quality of life for all people.

3

Groups in Remedial Treatment Settings

The purpose of this chapter is to define groups in remedial settings, such as outpatient, inpatient, and long-term residential treatment settings. The term *remedial* is defined as "tending to cure or restore to health" (*American Heritage Dictionary of the English Language*, 2009). Synonyms are alterative, curative, healing, sanative, and therapeutic. The term *remedial* is not typically used as a way to identify treatment settings; however, remediation as used in this chapter refers to the continuum of care from prevention to remediation/intervention to post-intervention (most commonly offered in terms of support or self-help groups). While settings that involve remediation would be expected only to have remedial or psychotherapy groups, the reality is that all types of groups as defined by Association for Specialists in Group Work (Wilson, Rapin, & Haley-Banez, 2000)—that is, psychotherapy, counseling, psychoeducation, and task groups—play a role in remedial settings. The actual implementation of these groups, however, is a different story. In our experience, the distinctions made between the types of groups in theory are rarely referred to as such in treatment settings, particularly in relation to "psychotherapy" or "counseling" groups. Nonetheless, in this chapter we have outlined the various types of groups and the forms in which they may be found in treatment settings.

Psychotherapy or Remedial Groups in Treatment Settings

Psychotherapy or remedial groups are generally aimed at personality reconstruction for serious psychological problems or distress (Wilson et al., 2000). Prospective members for therapy groups are generally screened and evaluated to determine eligibility, commitment, and ability to contribute to the group process. Psychotherapy groups are offered in health care settings, private practice, inpatient and outpatient treatment, and residential treatment centers. Participants of psychotherapy groups may deal with a range of issues, such as personality disorders, traumatic events, and interpersonal and developmental issues such as grief, substance abuse, depression, and eating disorders.

The ASGW training standards (Wilson et al., 2000) require a psychotherapy group facilitator to possess knowledge of the principles of normal and abnormal human development and functioning. These skills are acquired through training in group-based cognitive, affective, behavioral, or systematic intervention strategies. With this training, the facilitator is prepared to confront negative emotional arousal that addresses personal and interpersonal problems of living, to remediate perceptual and cognitive distortions or repetitive patterns of dysfunctional behavior, and promote personal and interpersonal growth and development. These core competencies are applied among people who may be experiencing severe and/or chronic maladjustment.

Psychotherapy groups help group members understand and remediate their *significant* emotional and psychological problems, focusing on intrapersonal and interpersonal dynamics (Yalom, 2005). The term *significant* helps define the difference between remedial and counseling types of groups. For example, in a residential treatment agency for adolescents, a resident may be experiencing significant loss of a parent recently killed in an automobile accident. The level of grief can be complicated by layers of unresolved problems, such as parental neglect, posttraumatic stress, and substance abuse. The resident is significantly impaired, experiencing health complaints, decreased functioning, and great psychiatric comorbidity (Elliott, Rivera, & Tucker, 2004). Psychotherapy groups can assist members with psychological disorders by providing safety, support, and a skilled therapist to navigate the complexity of issues.

Counseling Groups in Treatment Settings

Counseling groups can be included in remedial treatment settings to help participants resolve career, educational, personal, social, and developmental concerns through processes of interpersonal interaction, support, and problem solving (Conyne, 2000). These groups are generally for people who may be experiencing transitory maladjustment, who are at risk for the development of personal or interpersonal problems, or who seek enhancement of personal quality and abilities (Wilson et al., 2000). The goal of counseling is to encourage lifelong skills for adaptation and success in the community. Counseling is more interpersonally oriented than other formats and requires the skills of a facilitator extensively trained in psychological assessment and group counseling techniques. Counseling groups are problem centered and applied in the context of here-and-now interaction. This method is sometimes preferred when the therapist wants to help participants with psychological and social issues that impede and complicate adjustment. It is also preferred when therapists wish to help participants process emotional reactions or personality issues that may be apparent to the group (Elliott et al., 2004). The difference between remedial groups and counseling groups can be described in this grief and loss scenario: Counseling is used to increase the reality of loss, to help the group participant deal with expressed and latent affect and overcome various impediments to readjustment, and to encourage the client to make a healthy emotional withdrawal from the deceased and feel comfortable reinvesting in another relationship. Grief psychotherapy approach is often used when a group member fails to grieve or has trouble resolving feelings. The loss has become so overwhelming for the group member that he or she is impaired and unable to function.

_____ Psychoeducational Groups in Treatment Settings

Psychoeducational group work focuses on educating, preventing, and developing competencies through such structured groups as social skills, parenting, substance abuse, and life skills training (e.g., Gazda & Pistole, 1985). The application of principles of normal human development and functioning through group-based educational and developmental strategies occurs in the context of here-and-now interactions that promote personal and interpersonal growth and development and the prevention of future difficulties (Wilson et al., 2000). A psychoeducational format is best used among people who may be at risk for the development of personal or interpersonal problems or who seek enhancement of personal qualities and abilities.

The educational properties of a group may be the most rudimentary function of therapeutic group work. Unlike educational groups, which function primarily to convey useful information to members, psychoeducational groups address psychological content and leaders of these groups are sensitive to the potential effects of this content on members (Elliott et al., 2004). Psychoeducational groups can be effectively adapted to serve culturally diverse populations and can be tailored to people in their preferred language (Gallagher-Thompson, Arean, Rivera, & Thompson, 2001). The use of interdisciplinary teams in psychoeducational groups is also popular, allowing experts from different fields to work as cofacilitators (e.g., a nutritionist with a counselor, a nurse with a psychologist) to ensure that detailed and complex information is provided to participants (Elliott et al., 2004) in treatment settings.

_____ Task Groups in Treatment Settings

There is a distinct difference between task groups and psychotherapy groups; however, task groups are commonplace in some treatment centers, particularly in residential treatment settings. For instance, task groups are routinely used to prepare residents for their day. The purpose is to focus on applying group dynamic principles and processes to facilitate a smooth transition for residents. Task groups are instrumental as check-in groups providing an efficient and effective means to communicate information to the group. These groups offer structure, predictability, and problem solving. Task groups elicit information from the participants and are useful in identifying areas of concern. These groups can offer a sense of direction, a reminder of daily schedules, a place to vent frustrations, and an avenue to seek support. Addressing the group at specific times throughout the day provides an opportunity to communicate and revisit individual and collective group goals. Groups are more effective when members have common goals for the group and when they have a clear and shared sense of how these goals will be attained (Higginbotham, West, & Forsyth, 1988).

Group work in long-term residential treatment settings, however, is commonplace, because the residents are in constant communication with one another. Because they often function as a community, the dynamics of the *group milieu* are sometimes unique to that setting. In this next section, we will focus more specifically on groups in treatment settings.

Groups in Long-Term Residential Treatment

In the past, residential treatment centers were understood to involve orienting the daily lives of children in institutions around psychodynamic and other therapeutic principles. Youth counselors were assigned the duty of oversight during most activities, serving as primary therapeutic agents. Most residential programs would describe themselves as doing milieu therapy, but such ideas were seldom defined or applied in rigorous ways. More recently, there has been a paradigm shift in residential programs from behavioral management approaches to therapeutic interventions. I (Yozamp) have been a part of this change. Although family and individual therapy are provided by skilled therapists, the group milieu describes all interactions and activities in residential treatment as potentially therapeutic. These community interactions are subject to exploration and interpretation on a daily basis. Residents are encouraged to take responsibility for themselves and others within their environment.

Group therapists in residential settings hope that residents will not only obtain symptomatic relief but also alter their response to future crises. Residents are selected by admissions personnel, so therapists have little control over group composition. There is great heterogeneity of psychopathology in the group. Simplifying and focusing on realistic goals is important. It is obvious that talking helps these residents. Several residents have reported feeling less isolated with their problems when they learn that others share their same experiences. Therapists take on the role of "problem spotting" to help individuals learn about maladaptive interpersonal behavior. They help each resident identify major problem areas and encourage each to work on these areas in the future (Yalom, 2005).

Residential treatment facilities use the group milieu to encourage self reflection and change, however, dealing with differing levels of cognitive abilities and diagnoses can be a challenge. Children and adolescents face adversity such as maltreatment, abandonment, and enormous loss, creating a need for more sophisticated therapies to address the complexity of diagnosis. Most conceptualizations of group development are predicated on the belief that the group is closed, with unchanging membership. The findings of an exploratory study conducted by Schopler and Galinsky (1995) concluded that movement beyond beginnings is possible. However, the impact of open membership is likely to result in a more cyclical pattern of group development, with regression occurring when members enter and/or leave the group (Schopler & Galinsky, 1995). As Yalom (2005) has commented, this may impede the motivation and self-reflection quality of the group. The socialization that groups offer might be highly constraining and oppressive for some of the members; however, the intensity of the group milieu can be beneficial in that it is a daily ritual that offers a sense of commonality amongst its members.

Yalom (2005) rejects the idea that inpatient groups should be used to solve problems or reduce the symptoms associated with severe and persistent mental illness. Rather, the group functions to make the resident aware of the self and how the self interacts with others, identify problems for further therapeutic investigation, and introduce the concept that therapy can be helpful in achieving a more functional state of living (Emer, 2004). For example, individuals suffering from borderline personality disorder make up between 10% and 15% of inpatient psychiatric admissions and experience considerable interpersonal difficulties, often resulting in self-destructive behaviors (Emer, 2004). These individuals, oftentimes, are admitted to residential treatment centers. Stress aggravates and causes the individual to become disorganized, which can lead to hospitalization due to self-harm behaviors. Residential staff and inpatient hospital staff are often in communication, trying to best meet the needs of this population. Yalom's approach to this specific group holds merit, as the individual finds support in the group milieu but is encouraged to remain in the present to interact respectfully with others. Most members in counseling or therapy groups have conflicts within themselves, often stemming from unfinished business from the past. Helping members share an understanding of issues such as guilt, shame, abandonment, and low self-esteem reduces the stigma and feelings of worthlessness. This remains a daunting task.

Best Practices in Offering Groups in Treatment Settings

As noted in Chapter 2, best practices delineated by ASGW (Thomas & Pender, 2008) offer guidelines and a conceptual framework for the implementation of effective groups. These best practice guidelines are as follows:

1. Planning—the logistical tasks of assessing need, identifying group goals, setting group structure, determining resources, screening members, selecting facilitators, and the like

2. Performing—the adaptive implementation of the plan, generating meaning, and creating the therapeutic conditions necessary to maximize group experience

3. Processing—the reflective practice of processing group workings with members, supervisors, and colleagues, as well as evaluating process and outcome of the group

A more recent ASGW document, *Multicultural and Social Justice Competence Principles for Group Workers* (Singh, Merchant, Skudrzyk, & Ingene, 2012), provides guidelines on the integration of multicultural and social justice issues for each of these functions.

The target population for groups in treatment settings may already be established, such as clients in health care settings, inpatient and outpatient treatment, private practice, or residential treatment centers. Planning and screening are important to assess the clients' willingness to reflect on their interpersonal style and to make changes. Planning involves a needs assessment that considers the values and culture of existing members. The assessment may involve a review of clinical information and a client interview. Most important, group facilitators must be skilled in therapeutic strategies and group dynamics. A skilled group facilitator manages communication while balancing safety and member disclosure to protect other group members from physical, emotional, or psychological trauma. Groups in remedial settings such as hospitals, inpatient and outpatient settings, private practice, and residential treatment agencies often require an active style of leadership. Most groups in these settings need structure, organization, and direction. The group leader or facilitator is directive, with an understanding of the specific needs of the population guiding adjustment of group structure to meet those needs. The leader should encourage thought-provoking exchange and be willing to intervene when necessary.

Partnering with group members in developing the goals and design of the group is a critical step toward building ownership. Remedial groups require a confident facilitator knowledgeable in the subject matter and experienced with the population. Culture-specific understanding will enhance greater communication and appreciation of style differences. Depending on the multicultural context of the population served, groups may be structured in a way that best addresses the diversity needs of the group. Merchant (2006, 2009) has identified three types of diversity-related groups: (1) culture-specific groups (people who share a common experience as a result of their diversity), (2) intercultural learning groups (designed to promote cultural understanding across groups), and (3) other-content–focused groups (focused on other issues but consider diversity issues within the group). Therefore, a psychotherapy/remedial group offered in a residential treatment center for adolescents that is located in a predominantly White community may lack staff diversity to mirror the cultural backgrounds of the residents. A group facilitator will need to immerse him or herself in a particular cultural context to understand diversity issues. This will lead to culturally appropriate goals for the group and an understanding of different communication styles. Planned activities that are culturally grounded and relevant to the target population will be necessary to evaluate the success of the group.

Attention to intragroup differences as they relate to gender, age, sexual orientation, disability, culture/race/ethnicity, and other social statuses is necessary. This is especially true when facilitating sensitive topic groups in hospital settings, inpatient and outpatient settings, private practice, and residential treatment centers. Processing group dynamics with group members during sessions and among leaders between sessions is an important aspect of the learning process. Group enhances learning and promotes growth among members (Yalom, 2005). Similarly, leaders need to allow time between groups to process their experiences with one another and/or with supervisors or consultants.

A coordinated approach to group therapy requires communication between therapists and other staff members to make decisions about individual patients/residents. Competence with specific training in group process is the key to being an effective group facilitator. Some therapists interchange psychotherapy, psychoeducation, counseling, and task-related styles to facilitate effective groups. No matter what the strategy, special attention to planning and assessing group members will enhance the therapeutic potential of groups.

Best practice is in place when there is effective evaluation. Group termination requires closure to address concerns and to provide ongoing support. Evaluation is an essential part of group work in that it empowers the group members to share their insight, suggest improvements, and receive ongoing support. Group members provide valuable feedback in reference to their experience in group.

Research on Effectiveness of Groups in Treatment Settings

Although groups in remedial treatment settings are cost-effective, many practitioners are concerned about their efficacy (Emer, 2004). To be an effective and relevant group worker in today's world, a counselor needs to first develop basic knowledge and skills in group work. Most counselor education programs should be providing this training as a matter of course. In addition, specializing in a certain type of group work requires the practitioner to obtain training and supervision that build on the core competencies. Many counselor education programs are able to provide such training now, or are gearing up to do so. However, it also is important for the counseling practitioner who is interested in group work to seek additional training and supervision through appropriate continuing education services, such as group work offerings sponsored by the American Counseling Association or ASGW (Conyne, 2000).

Further quantitative research is needed to determine which groups work best for specific inpatient populations (Delucia-Waack, Gerrity, Kalodner, & Riva, 2004). What impedes this process in residential treatment is the difficulty of separating out the impact of various treatment approaches on individuals. Residents who participate in a particular form of group treatment are also living together and working with different professionals (occupational therapists, recreation therapists, school psychologists, unit therapists, psychiatrists, and mental health practitioners). In addition, the population is often too unstable to study. This is the reason why so many inpatient group practitioners have advocated for a single-session format to accomplish treatment goals. However, populations at risk for continued intensified harm, pain, dysfunction, or unmet needs can benefit from a group to gain skills, understanding, and emotional learning to reduce their vulnerability (Greif & Ephross, 2005).

In contrast to outpatient therapists, inpatient therapists do not have the luxury of identifying major interpersonal problems, working through the meaning of these interpersonal symptoms with a patient, and then overseeing the process of change (Yalom, 1983). The great majority of patients/ residents in inpatient settings are in crisis, and they search for comfort and survival rather than growth. Clustering at the top of every therapist's hierarchy of values are such qualities as personal growth, self-knowledge, and self-actualization. The inpatient therapist must help lay the foundation of safety and security and leave the architecture and masonry of the upper stories and spires to the therapist who will treat the patient after discharge (Yalom, 1983).

As interest in group processes and group dynamics developed and accelerated (most particularly since the 1980s) the research base of the area strengthened. Not unexpectedly, the main arenas for the exploration of groups, and for building theory about them, have continued to be sociology and social psychology. Perhaps the most obvious is work, and the contexts and practices of teams. But it has also acted as a spur to development in those fields of education, therapy, social care, and social action that use groups to foster change.

There is a call for deepening the focus of research to cover a comprehensive set of variables, link process with outcome, increase sample sizes, and apply the findings to practice and training of group specialists (DeLucia-Waack et al., 2004). With regard to practice, new and innovative techniques need to be encouraged and must continue to be developed. Systematic descriptions of interventions that have been proven effective have begun to be published, but there is much room for innovation and growth in the field. In regard to research, more studies are needed, with larger samples, rigorous designs, and diverse populations (DeLucia-Waack et al., 2004). Training and continuing education for groups across the life span, in different settings, and with different therapeutic goals are essential to help facilitators select effective interventions.

Most research focuses on the effectiveness of group work, not what makes groups effective (Delucia-Waack, 1997). Delucia-Waack ponders the following questions as the subject of future research and theory: How do certain aspects of the group environment encourage self-disclosure? How can leaders facilitate such a group environment? How do personality variables interact with group environment factors?

Example of a Trauma-Focused Group in a Residential Treatment Setting

Trauma-focused cognitive behavioral therapy (TF-CBT) is one among several approaches currently being used in residential settings, and one being used in the setting in which I (Yozamp) work. Many individuals admitted to residential treatment centers have a history of trauma. TF-CBT is an evidence-based treatment approach that provides a rich array of practice skills to reduce anxiety associated with trauma (Cohen, Mannarino, & Deblinger, 2006). These skills can be in the form of visual imagery, deep breathing, relaxation exercises, journaling, or sensory supports. The resident supported by the therapist takes several sessions to create his or her story through pictures or written words. The story includes positive memories as well as difficult times. As the narrative story unfolds, the therapist is separately working with the resident's "witness" in preparation to hear the story. The witness is often the parent but can be any significant person in the life of the resident. When the resident is ready and his or her "witness" is prepared to hear the story, the narrative is read in its entirety. The prepared witness supports the resident during the reading. The eventual process of overexposure leads to symptom reduction.

Due to the success of TF-CBT therapy, a group addressing trauma was formed to meet the needs of female residents in the treatment setting where I worked. The need for a gender-specific group was identified by the female residents themselves, many of whom had experienced sexual abuse. Group members were screened and referred to the group by their respective individual therapists. The group consisted of six girls aged 12 to 17 and was cofacilitated by two female staff therapists trained in TF-CBT. The group was offered as a psychotherapy/counseling group for 8 weeks. A common experience that many of the group members shared was the shame associated with their past experiences, which was often expressed through self-harm and aggression. Several other issues were also addressed as they emerged—for example, cutting, anger, relationship issues, lack of trust, and difficulties with males, particularly those in authority. Through the careful use of repeated imagining of the traumatic experience, within the controlled safety of the group, members were taught to gain control of the overwhelming emotions associated with the event. In addition to retelling the trauma, group members were exposed to and taught coping skills such as cognitive restructuring, stress inoculation, relapse prevention, and social skills (Foy, Eriksson, & Trice, 2001). No formal evaluation was conducted; however, members reported that the group encouraged them to look inside of themselves, understand the connection between emotional pain and behavior, and stop blaming themselves. They further commented that it is easier to discuss past sexual abuse with other female residents. TF-CBT is an evidence-based practice measuring outcomes in reduction of symptoms and is thus instrumental in the treatment of trauma-related cases. The combination of individual and group therapy provides a sense of universality for the participants, helping residents realize that others share their experiences and struggles. Knowing that others have experienced similar trauma can decrease feelings of alienation.

Example of a Psychoeducational Group in a Day Treatment Setting

An example of a psychoeducational group in an outpatient setting can be seen in a local intensive day treatment program for children and adolescents who experience significant emotional and behavioral difficulties in their homes and communities. Local students in grades 1 through 12 who are experiencing emotional and behavioral difficulties, after traditional educational or therapeutic interventions have been unsuccessful, may access this program run by a multidisciplinary team. The day-treatment setting helps youth returning from a partial hospital, inpatient hospital, or residential treatment transition to a less restrictive environment. Clinical services are provided by a team that includes a program manager, clinical supervisor, program supervisor, EBD (emotional and behavioral disorder) classroom teachers, paraprofessional teaching assistants, mental health practitioners, therapists, and skills counselors. This outpatient setting provides a highly structured environment for individual and group interventions to respond to the unique challenges of educating at-risk students who have not found success in a traditional classroom or alternative setting. The goal of the program is to help the children and adolescents function more effectively in their day-to-day lives, such as at home, with child-care providers, and in school settings. Educational needs are identified through strength-based assessments conducted by the educational and mental health professionals to determine each student's abilities, interests, aptitudes, and values. These assessments create a learning environment that focuses on interests, abilities, and the student's own personal vision for the future. Family participation is an integral and vital part of a student's success. An individual treatment plan is developed for each child that includes measurable short-term social, coping, and recreational goals, as well as longer-term mental health goals to help the child succeed in the development of emotional, social, and learning behaviors. By understanding the influences of the environment on behavior, as well as the strengths and weaknesses of the student, professionals can better develop a positive behavior-change program. This evidence-based practice measures progress or identifies the need to change treatment goals.

I (Yozamp) visited this day-treatment center to learn more about the programs and observe a psychoeducational group referred to as the "morning group" for children aged 7 to 9 in the intensive day treatment program. Children are placed in the group following the various assessments determining need and appropriateness for the program. The group, consisting of about eight children, provides a time for transitioning students from home back to the program. The facilitator structures the group through various activities, which involve art, play, stories, and other interactive tasks. On the day I observed the group, the facilitator invited the students to share how their evening had gone the previous day. One student was upset about something that occurred at home, while another student did not sleep well. Both students were concerned that their evenings would have a negative effect on their days. The facilitator asked group members to break into dyads and brainstorm various outcomes for how their days could unfold. The group was able to link thoughts, feelings, and behavior using a cognitive approach. I witnessed the positive energy in the room as students were engaged and supportive of one another. The group processed their activity, offering positive and negative responses to how their days would unfold. The group ended with an exercise video, which simply provided movement to elevate their mood. Group therapy occurs daily with students, while family and individual services are offered on a weekly basis.

In summary, groups are facilitated by skilled educators and mental health professionals, with a high staff-to-student ratio. Evidence-based practices are implemented to measure outcomes of treatment. Behaviors are redirected in a respectful manner to avoid shame and to keep students on task. Reminders are constantly used to help students adhere to group guidelines. One of the fundamental pillars of good psychotherapy is timing; there are times when the resident/patient can make good use of insights, and there are times when he or she is not yet able to hear or integrate interpretations (Yalom, 1983). Understanding this helps the therapist attend to the therapeutic work that is possible in the group.

Conclusion

Training in group work is beginning to catch up with its practice in the field and with demands from consumers for more groups and a wider variety of groups. The ASGW professional training standards are intended to assist in this effort. Counselors are becoming better prepared to offer and lead a comprehensive range of personal change and task groups. This evolution should lead to group work being used more effectively in a wider array of human settings.

Considerable insights into the process and functioning of groups can be gained via the literature of group dynamics and small groups. Of particular help are explorations of group structure (including group size and the roles people play), group norms and culture, group goals, and the relative cohesiveness of groups. That said, the skills needed for engaging in and with group life—and the attitudes, orientations, and ideas associated with them—are learned, predominantly, through experiencing group life. This provides a powerful rationale for educative interventions.

4

Support Groups and Self-Help Groups

In a recent NBC comedy called *Go On,* the protagonist has experienced a major loss in his life (the accidental death of his young wife) and is asked to seek out a support group to address his grief and loss. While the show highlights the importance of the support group in dealing with his loss, it also unfortunately feeds into misinformation and stereotypes about how support groups are facilitated. Nevertheless, this show demonstrates the need and acceptance of support groups for people dealing with various stressors and transitions in life. In this chapter, we highlight the use of groups as sources for support and self-help—as part of the continuum of care from prevention to remediation to support.

In the helping profession, the term *support* implies providing people who are dealing with some level of distress or dysfunction with "material and non-material resources as comfort, encouragement, advice, and environmental manipulation" (Pearson, 1983, p. 362). Based on this perspective, support and self-help groups may serve the function of providing assistance to those who are already suffering or preventing them from experiencing further distress or dysfunction. As such, support and self-help groups may serve as an adjunct for ongoing treatment, after care, relapse prevention, or simply as a forum for people experiencing the same problem to come together to develop a supportive community. Traditionally, the notion of self-help and support groups was viewed somewhat tentatively, and even with hostility, by helping professionals. However, the mushrooming of self-help and support groups in the past four decades has been a force to reckon with, leading to recognition of their usefulness in addition to counseling and therapy, or even as the sole form of mental health delivery (Riordan & Beggs, 1987). The rise of the self-help and support group movement points to an immense unmet need in relationship to interacting with "fellow sufferers," as well as providing a means for transference of knowledge to problem solving and a platform for advocacy (Kurtz, 1997).

What Are Support and Self-Help Groups, and How Are They Different From Counseling and Therapy Groups?

The terms *support* and *self-help* are often blurred, sometimes seen as one and the same, and other times viewed as distinct forms of help. The waters have been muddied further by the evolving nature and expanded use of self-help and support groups in the past four decades. The increased use of technology, the advent of managed-care systems, and the abundance of such groups in the medical, educational, and psychological fields have changed the availability of and access to resources. Even so, some defining features may distinguish the different types of groups.

A self-help group, according to Kurtz (1997), is a *"supportive, educational, usually change-oriented mutual-aid group that addresses a single life problem or condition shared by all members"* (p. 4). Leadership may emerge rather than being designated. Generally, members, including the group leader, are experiencing or have experienced conditions or difficulties that brought the group together (Riordan & Beggs, 1987). Professionals are seldom involved in leading the groups unless they are members. Groups are often structured and involve specific methods of help in ameliorating the problem or condition. The purpose of the self-help group may be to bring about change at the individual and/or societal level (Kurtz, 1997). Members of the group may see themselves as participating in their own care, with long-time members seeing great value in donating their time and service for the benefit of others (*Encyclopedia of Mental Disorders*, 2013). Silverman (2002) contends that self-help may be a misnomer, as both helper and helpee in this situation are equally benefited. As such, the term *mutual aid* may be more appropriate for this form of group. Several differences have been identified between self-help and therapy groups (Kurtz, 1997; Riordan & Beggs, 1987).

1. Self-help groups tend to have a single topic or focus (e.g., Alcoholics Anonymous or Parents Anonymous), whereas counseling and therapy groups may have a more global focus.

2. The primary focus in self-help groups may be information and guidance, whereas addressing interpersonal relationships, growth, and deeper-level issues may be the focus of counseling and therapy groups.

3. While self-help groups may also focus on personal change, the group experience itself does not focus on "here-and-now" interactions among members as a therapeutic technique in counseling groups.

4. The leaders of self-help groups are likely to be lay helpers, whereas counseling groups would have professionally trained helpers.

5. Self-help groups and counseling groups may differ in their size, cost, meeting place, and number of sessions.

6. Self-help groups tend to adhere to a specific ideology in the definition and intervention of the problem, whereas counseling groups adopt a variety of theories and intervention methods.

Support groups, on the other hand, are defined as groups that provide *"emotional support and information to persons with a common problem"* (Kurtz, 1997, p. 4) and are viewed on a wide spectrum of informality versus formality. Support groups may range from being loose informal structures that provide a healing environment and are led by lay persons (*Encyclopedia of Mental Disorders*, 2013) to more structured groups connected with an agency or larger organization and led by professionals (Kurtz, 1997). The primary goals of emotional support and education may supersede those of personal transformation, advocacy, and societal change. Groups may be smaller in size, may be less structured, and may or may not involve some form of financial compensation for the leaders (Kurtz, 1997). Some support groups may have an open format whereby members can attend based on convenience and need, while others may be structured, closed groups with defined membership. In some cases, support groups may be started as counseling groups and evolve into a support group. Self-help groups may also serve as a support group for some. If viewed on a continuum, self-help groups may be seen on one end of the continuum, with counseling and therapy groups on the other and support groups somewhere in between (Schopler & Galinsky, 1995).

Despite the many attempts to distinguish support, self-help, and counseling or therapy groups, they continue to be confused. Oftentimes, the terms *support* and *self-help* are used interchangeably, with self-help groups being referred to as support groups and vice versa. In cases where there is a true overlap of the groups, they may be better referred to as *hybrid* groups (Kurtz, 1997). I (Merchant) have had experience with one such hybrid group. Some of us in our community decided to come together to address the difficulties our children were facing in predominantly White K–12 school systems, and we formed the Parents of Children of Color group. We invited community members who had similar experiences to come together to share their stories. This group not only helped mobilize us to address issues at a larger systemic level (by inviting school principals, teachers, and superintendents to the meetings) but also helped validate our experiences. This group was peer-led, with somewhat ambiguous goals; however, the end result was that it helped empower us to take action. This group, which initially began as a support group, grew into an advocacy group. I quickly realized that my group-facilitation skills came in handy in helping group members navigate emotional and sometimes conflict- and tension-filled moments. Such organic groups that grow out of a specific need in the community may morph into different forms depending on the emergent issues of the group. Sometimes the label attached to the group "is not what it is, but what will make it attractive to potential members" (Pearson, 1983, p. 362). Given the confusion, it may be helpful to trace the development of both support and self-help groups here.

History: Statistics/Demographics on the Number of Support and Self-Help Groups

The rise of self-help movements can be traced to the role social workers played in the 19th century in helping new immigrants with settlement difficulties (Riordan & Beggs, 1987). As the field of psychology began to focus more on social and applied issues, adjustment and emotional difficulties were relegated to mental health professionals. The growth in self-help movements is attributed in part to the frustration of the public with the ineffectiveness and dehumanization of formal health care systems (Riordan & Beggs, 1987). As stated earlier, the self-help movement was initially met with resistance by mental health professionals. The resistance occurred for a variety of reasons—namely, the concern for lack of leadership skills in group dynamics, the neglect of mental health care, and perhaps even the fear of being usurped by the self-help movement. Over the years, however, there has been a greater acceptance of self-help groups serving as an adjunct to the therapeutic process. With the increase in attention to prevention health, professionals see the use of self-help groups as improving the outcome of ongoing or future treatment (Riordan & Beggs, 1987).

The past four decades have seen an increase in the self-help and support group movement. In the 1970s, the annual rate of growth in self-help groups was about 3%. In the 1980s, the annual growth was estimated at 8.4%. It was predicted that by the year 2000 there would be more than 10 million users of self-help groups (see Kurtz, 1997). In 1996, the largest self-help group, Alcoholics Anonymous, reported 1,307,803 individual members and 58,084 groups in the United States and Canada. In 2013, the number of Alcoholics Anonymous groups had reached a total of 65,916, with 1,425,647 individual members (Alcoholics Anonymous, 2013).

Internet usage has vastly changed the landscape for accessing support and self-help groups. Earlier, helping professionals relied primarily on handing out brochures or printed information. Now, with the help of the Internet, consumers can instantly access information on a plethora of resources. Several clearinghouses have been developed to help people find the right types of support groups and self-help groups. Self-help clearinghouses exist in several states, and national clearinghouses such as the American Self-Help Group Clearinghouse (2013) provide web-based and telephone support for finding the right resources. The latter also provides a database of more than a 1,000 national, international, model, and online self-help support groups for a variety of stressful life situations—including mental health, addiction, bereavement, parenting, abuse, and more. The resources are alphabetized and can be easily found at the local, national, and international levels. These websites also provide information on how to form a local self-help/support group if none is available.

Types of Self-Help Groups

Self-help groups are initiated in a variety of ways and for many reasons. Two long-standing self-help groups are Alcoholics Anonymous and Recovery International. Alcoholics Anonymous began in the 1930s through the efforts of Bill Wilson and Dr. Bob Smith, both of whom were struggling with compulsive alcohol use. After successfully receiving help from a quasi-religious/spiritual group (Oxford Group), they began to look for other problem drinkers to share their story with. They eventually formed their own independent program, borrowing from the spiritual principles of the Oxford Group, as well as from other entities that made sense in terms of their personal experiences. They published their first book, *Alcoholics Anonymous,* in 1939, and this ultimately became the name of the group. Since then, Alcoholics Anonymous has grown tremendously, with the latest statistics showing 65,916 registered groups and 1,425,647 individual members in the United States and Canada (Alcoholics Anonymous, 2013). The Alcoholics Anonymous movement gave rise to scores of 12-step programs, such as Al-Anon and Alateen (for friends and family of alcoholics) and Narcotics Anonymous, and programs that go beyond substance abuse, such as Emotions Anonymous (recovery from mental and emotional illness), Overeaters Anonymous, and Workoholics Anonymous.

Recovery International (previously known as Recovery Inc.), on the other hand, was started in 1937 by Abraham Low, a psychiatrist from Chicago. His original aim was to provide outpatient groups to his patients who had completed treatment and were discharged in the community. Unfortunately, his attempts toward relapse prevention and education were viewed unfavorably by the medical community, forcing him to abandon his efforts. To his surprise, the group continued to meet, leading him to write the text *Mental Health Through Will Training*, which has become the core of Recovery International's program. Recovery International became an independent organization in 1952 and has grown to 600 community meetings in the United States and internationally (Recovery International, 2013).

Alcoholics Anonymous and Recovery International are examples of change-oriented associations (Kurtz, 1997)—that is, associations that promote individual and societal change. Another example of a change-oriented program is Parents Anonymous Inc., a child-abuse prevention program that was started by a potentially abusive mother, Jolly K. (see Parents Anonymous, 2012). Other self-help groups have support and education as their primary goals—for example, the National Alliance on Mental Illness (2012), designed to help those affected by mental illness; The Compassionate Friends, a group for those who are grieving the death of a child; Candlelighters, for children who have cancer and their parents; Alzheimer's Disease and Related Disorders Association; and Weight Watchers.

What all these self-help groups have in common is that they are established organizations with a specific organizational structure and a particular ideology and worldview that define their respective group. The narrative of the organization tends to influence the narrative of the individual. For example, Kurtz (1997) states, "As the organization's story becomes a part of one's identity, one's own story, a person comes to understand his or her identity in that story" (p. 11). Kurtz further reports that the self-help movement in essence mobilizes the ethos of "self-determination, self-reliance, self-production, and self-empowerment" (p. 11) by tapping into the resources of the individual, group, and community. The role of professional helpers in relationship to these groups may vary from playing a leadership role as a board member in the organization to serving as a consultant, organizer, facilitator, linker, or supporter of the group (Kurtz, 1997). Support groups, on the other hand, may be very different in size, makeup, and intent, with the role of professionals sometimes being more direct and hands-on than in self-help groups.

Support groups are traditionally smaller in size and are generally affiliated with an agency or a larger, formal organization. As stated earlier, support groups are designed to provide emotional support and education related to a common problem, with behavioral and societal change being a less important goal. Support groups do not provide therapy but may be psychoeducational or educational in nature with "therapeutic moments," as described by a support group facilitator (Fuchs-Hoesch, personal communication, November 1, 2012). While the groups may be facilitated by professionals, there may be greater emphasis on peer help—a characteristic that overlaps with self-help groups. According to Pearson (1983), the role of support groups may vary from serving a "remedial" role (moving people from dysfunctional to more effective ways of functioning) to an "effectiveness maintenance and enhancement view," which emphasizes prevention and interventions that support effective developmental progress.

A support group can be initiated for any number of reasons based on the need in the agency, organization, or community. Agency-based groups may be more specific to the types of services provided. Hospitals and local community counseling centers may offer groups as a supplement to individual and family counseling, or as after-care or ongoing support programs for those dealing with mental illness, substance abuse, or HIV/AIDS. Chemical dependency centers may offer ongoing after-care support groups for those who have received inpatient and outpatient treatment. Community agencies such as churches, domestic violence shelters, and sexual assault centers often offer in-house or outreach support groups in the local community and schools to provide emotional support, education, and advocacy. Job centers may offer support groups as a vehicle to address issues related to job loss. Veterans Affairs and other local centers offer support groups for veterans, an ever-increasing need due to the number of returning veterans from the Iraq and Afghanistan wars, not to mention the continued need for support for veterans from the Vietnam and earlier wars. Counseling centers on college campuses offer numerous support groups, providing support to nontradi-tional students and assisting those with test anxiety, depression, eating dis-orders, or relationship issues, for example. Furthermore, various units on college campuses, such as the women's center, LGBT services, and multicul-tural student services, may offer more culture-specific groups to support LGBT students, students of color, survivors of sexual violence, and more. Similarly, support groups may be established in K–12 schools—for example, groups for children of divorced parents, for bullying prevention, or for enhancing relationship skills.

Creating such support groups in larger institutions helps provide a safety net for those who are suffering or those who just need a support network. I (Merchant) have been involved in facilitating a number of support groups, including the previously mentioned grassroots community effort that brought parents of children of color together in the community, groups addressing issues faced by our children in the public schools, and groups for children and adolescents of color in school, community, and residential treat-ment settings.

Therapeutic Forces in Support and Self-Help Groups

Yalom (2005) identified 11 therapeutic factors that contribute to an effective group experience. While these therapeutic factors were mostly in relation-ship to counseling and therapy groups, several studies have identified specific factors in play in self-help and support groups. Based on a review of the research, Kurtz (1997) identified five therapeutic factors that may appear in support and self-help groups—namely, *giving support, imparting informa-tion, conveying a sense of belonging, communicating experiential knowl-edge*, and *teaching coping methods. Giving support* is the overarching factor that encompasses most of the other factors, and it includes a sense of community, creating hope, getting factual information, and building self-confidence. Positive experiences in support groups were reported to be cor-related with greater supportive help-giving and guidance (Kurtz, 1997). The second therapeutic factor, *imparting information,* was considered equally important. Members often rely on obtaining accurate information through support and self-help groups. For instance, many of the larger organization-ally based self-help groups, such as National Alliance on Mental Illness and Parents Anonymous, provide various resources such as newsletters and bibliographies or invite outside experts to speak at their meetings. Similarly, the third factor, *conveying a sense of belonging,* helps re-create natural support systems such as those obtained through families and religious organizations. The fourth factor, *communicating experiential knowledge*, although not one of the therapeutic factors Yalom identified, is found to play a significant role in support and self-help groups. Experiential knowledge is often communicated via storytelling, when members share what things were like, how they joined the group, and the ways their lives have improved. In some groups (e.g., Alcoholics Anonymous), this process is ritualized, while in others it may be more informal. This storytelling may lead to the final therapeutic factor, *teaching coping methods*. Members learn from one another and experts specific ways they can better cope with whatever it is they are seeking help for (Kurtz, 1997).

Incorporating Best Practices in Support Groups

The categorization of groups in the Association for Specialists in Group Work (ASGW) training standards (Wilson, Rapin, & Haley-Banez, 2000) into task, psychoeducational, counseling, and psychotherapy doesn't allow for a clear demarcation of where support groups fit best. The amorphous and varied nature of self-help and support groups, coupled with the lack of attention or silent treatment toward support groups in the counseling and therapy literature, may compound some of the confusion in categorization. Based on the current definitions, support groups may straddle psychoeducational and counseling groups, as both include principles of normal human development; educational, developmental, and systemic strategies; personal and interpersonal growth; and prevention of future difficulties. The added dimension of helping people with "transitory maladjustment" (Wilson et al., 2000) in the categorization of counseling groups could perhaps be applied to support groups. In a critique of the previous ASGW categorization of groups in 1992, Waldo and Bauman (1998) suggest the inclusion of a continuum of goals in addressing *guidance, counseling,* and *therapy* groups. The goals include *development, remediation,* and *adjustment* as the three dimensions to be considered on a continuum of care (see Waldo & Bauman, 1998, for a more detailed discussion). The inclusion of "adjustment" goals in the ASGW categories would provide a better fit for a categorization of support groups, as it implies providing support and teaching coping mechanisms to people who are already dealing with a life problem or condition. The reason this becomes important is because the ASGW training standards define the training requirements and the type of knowledge and skills that encompass the scope of practice for group workers. The lack of specific training standards for leading support groups leaves a hole in the training of group workers and inadvertently perpetuates the notion that support groups do not require skilled facilitators.

Despite the lack of attention in training standards, the ASGW *Best Practice Guidelines* (Thomas & Pender, 2009), and *Multicultural and Social Justice Competence Principles* (Singh, Merchant, Skudrzyk, & Ingene, 2012) for group workers can apply equally to the planning, implementation, and facilitation of support groups. As stated in earlier chapters, the *Best Practice Guidelines*, as defined by ASGW (Thomas & Pender, 2008), incorporate the three Ps (i.e., planning, performing, and processing). Many of the same steps identified in the previous two chapters also apply to facilitating support groups and self-help groups, especially those that are smaller in size. The sometimes amorphous nature of support groups, however, creates unique challenges in the planning and implementation of such groups. The best practices discussed below pertain more to smaller-sized support groups than to the organizationally based self-help groups (such as 12-step groups), as meeting structure and planning may vary considerably in the latter. Outlined below are specific issues that may arise in conducting support groups.

Planning

Planning, as described by ASGW best practices (Thomas & Pender, 2008), involves many aspects, including assessment of group facilitator competency, ecological assessment of community needs and resources, and the specific tasks of recruiting, screening, establishing leadership roles, and deciding on format and evaluation of the groups. The degree of planning may differ based on whether the group structure is more formal or informal, the type of setting it emerges in—that is, agency or institution versus community— and the type of leadership—that is, whether led by professionals, paraprofessionals, or peers. Below, we discuss some of the steps that may come into play in planning for a support group.

The formal assessment of needs and structured planning for support groups may be more evident in agency- or institution-based support groups. Support groups in such settings may emerge as a result of a need to provide continued support to a group of clients who share a similar problem or from the clients themselves, who feel the need for ongoing support. Take, for example, a weekly support group that was established in our local Veterans Affairs hospital to provide community outreach and education for Vietnam veterans who had completed a 12-step program for chemical dependency and had comorbid issues related to depression, anxiety, and posttraumatic stress disorder (described in detail at the end of the chapter). This group grew out of a need for the agency to provide ongoing services, as well as from the veterans' need for a support network to aid in their recovery. Support groups may also emerge out of a needs assessment by a particular agency or institution that identifies a predominance of a certain problem within its setting, or where constituents report feeling neglected or isolated by their issues. For example, counseling centers on university campuses often offer relationship-oriented groups for those experiencing challenges in their

interpersonal relationships, academic support groups to improve study hab-
its and grades, or groups to provide support for nontraditional-aged students who feel overlooked by the university. Groups that grow out of the
efforts of an agency or institution are perhaps more likely to involve structured planning, with leadership involving professionals and paraprofessionals within the agency, especially if resources are allocated for such services.

On the other end of the continuum are informal, member-led groups that
grow out of grassroots efforts by community members to create a support
network for themselves. Informal groups are especially evident in minority
and disenfranchised communities as a result of the shared experience of
oppression, as well as the difficulties with support systems that cater primarily to the majority culture (Blustein, 1982). The development of such groups
has an empowering effect both on the members and the community. Take,
for instance, the support group established by immigrant parents whose
children were experiencing difficulty within the school system. As mentioned
previously, I (Merchant) was a member and coleader of a grassroots group
within our community. Our membership was open and mainly served as an
information-sharing support network for parents of color who were experiencing difficulties in navigating the school system. Leadership was on a
volunteer basis and changed as time went on, based on the availability of
members who could facilitate the group. There were no resources initially
available for our group; however, as the group progressed, it was evident
that we needed funding to provide food, transportation, and child care, as
many of the parents did not have access to these amenities. Resources were
eventually sought through grant funding and with the help of volunteers.
This group was not sustained over time, due to lack of formal structure as
well as dwindling interest and availability among the members.

Regardless of the type of group—formal or informal—partnering with
target populations is an important step in the development of the group.
Such partnering can be done in the predevelopment of the group or by inviting ongoing evaluation from members and providing adjustment of services
as the group progresses. Partnering with the target population allows for
cultural needs to be addressed, as well as involving and engaging the community, thereby creating a reciprocal and respectful relationship. I (Merchant)
learned firsthand the usefulness of partnering with the community—and the
many cultural issues in play when deciding on the location of the meetings—
when the local sexual assault center asked me to facilitate a group for
women of color. The sexual assault center had learned over time that it was
better able to provide information and support to women of color by providing a general support group rather than one specific to sexual issues.
Since the request came from the sexual assault center, I offered to lead the
group within its premises. I learned quickly that the sexual assault center
was not a comfortable location, and many of the women resisted attending
the group there. Based on the feedback from the participants, we moved the
group to a local Native American Center, which was perceived as being

"neutral" with regard to discussing sexual issues, and this generated much better attendance among group members.

Deciding on the type of group leadership is another important step in the planning process. Leadership in support groups may be member only, professional only, or equally shared by a professional and a member of the group (Kurtz, 1997). Support groups are generally based on members experiencing a shared problem; hence, group leaders, first and foremost, need to have a deeper level of knowledge and understanding of the issues to be addressed. So, for instance, a support group for sexual abuse survivors would need to be led by individuals who are knowledgeable about sexual violence and trauma related to such violence. Facilitators of such a group may be a professional working at a sexual assault center and a coleader who is a survivor of sexual violence. Groups can also be peer led, which may result from a member emerging as a leader or being designated by group members or rotation of leadership among the members. Regardless of whether the group is led by a professional, paraprofessional, or member, *a common mistake is the assumption that knowledge about the issues is sufficient for facilitating a group*. Best practice principles in facilitating groups involve *knowledge, experience,* and *competency*, in addition to knowledge about the focal topic. In the zeal to start support groups, ad hoc groups in particular may not recognize the importance of group facilitation skills.

Cultural competency is an important aspect of group facilitation skills. The type of leadership knowledge and skills may vary depending on the type of group—that is, whether it is a culture-specific group or other-content–focused group (Merchant, 2006, 2009). Facilitators of *culture-specific* groups, such as a support group for LGBT students on a college campus, would require working knowledge of the issues faced by the LGBT community and the level of credibility among the population served (Chojnacki & Gelberg, 1995; Merchant, 2006, 2009). Furthermore, facilitators of the LGBT support group would need to be knowledgeable about intragroup differences among the members—for example, the experience of LGBT students of color or the gender bias experienced by lesbians versus gays. Similarly, cultural competency is equally important in *other-content–focused* groups. Take, for instance, a support group for parents who are grieving the loss of a child that has varying ethnic and racial diversity membership. In addition to knowledge about grief and loss, facilitators need to know how to navigate differing communication styles, varying levels of cultural identity development, and the different cultural and religious practices in mourning the death of a family member.

The next step in planning is determining whether the group will have open or closed membership. More often than not, support groups tend to have open membership. The group starts with a core set of members from the population for whom the group is intended, with additional members being added as older members leave the group. The mix of old and new members not only allows for experiential knowledge to be passed on but also promotes stability and longevity (Kurtz, 1997). On the other hand, some groups are closed-ended and may be offered for a limited time. For example, our local sexual assault center offers such support groups for teenage girls who are survivors of sexual assault. The group is structured as a psychoeducational group with a closed membership and offered for 12 weeks at a time. Members of the group may choose to continue on in future groups if they feel the need for additional support.

Deciding on the type of membership, size, time, and location of the group are other logistical tasks that need to be completed. Membership may be homogenous, as in the case of the group for male Vietnam War veterans recovering from chemical dependency, or heterogeneous, as may be the case for a support group for nontraditional college students that includes member variability in age, gender, and a broad range of issues, with the common thread of "nontraditional" being the only defining factor. An ideal size for small support groups is generally recommended at 8 to 12 active members, as large groups become cumbersome to facilitate (Kurtz, 1997). Additional issues such as location and time should be decided based on the best fit for members, as cited previously in the example of the group for women of color. Recruitment of members may be achieved through flyers, referrals, electronic communication, and word of mouth. The level of screening may vary depending on the structure and nature of the support group, but screening is always advisable to ensure appropriateness of members for inclusion and to provide an opportunity to orient potential members to group goals and norms (Schopler & Galinsky, 1995). As recommended in the *Multicultural and Social Justice Competence Principles for Group Workers* (Singh et al., 2012), screening also provides the opportunity to ensure diversity of membership, attention to whether a person would be the "only one" from a particular minority group, and conversations related to norms regarding diversity in the group.

Performing and Processing

The ASGW *Best Practice Guidelines* (Thomas & Pender, 2008), while it does not specifically mention support groups, emphasizes the need for group leaders to be adequately trained and skilled in facilitating groups. According to Frew (1986), a highly functioning mutual support group would be able to appropriately address "each member's basic needs for comfort, safety, and affiliation and will eventually evolve into a cohesive community capable of dealing with the specific needs of the participant" (p. 93). He argues that professional leadership is needed to accomplish these goals. The reality, however, is that support groups may be facilitated by a leader who is not professionally trained, pointing to the need for professional organizations such as ASGW to develop guidelines and best practices specific to support groups. The therapeutic factors present in support groups, as discussed earlier in the chapter, are focused more on providing emotional support and information and assisting with coping skills; nonetheless, group facilitators need to know how to facilitate the development of mutual support between members and use interventions that are appropriate to the group process and development. Frew identifies three phases in the development of a support group: *inclusion* (addressing acceptance, safety, and belonging), *control* (negotiating power, identity, and authority), and *affection* (developing trust and intimacy). He recommends that group facilitators be knowledgeable about how to anticipate and respond to group members in each of these phases in the group.

Skilled group facilitation also necessitates cultural competency on the part of group leaders. The ASGW *Multicultural and Social Justice Competence Principles* (Singh et al., 2012) delineate the need for group facilitators to have awareness, knowledge, and skill in addressing a variety of cultural issues in the group, such as establishing norms that value cultural difference, negotiating differences in cultural and racial identity development, responding to language preferences, and ensuring that frameworks and techniques used are culturally grounded and appropriate. Furthermore, social justice advocacy skills such as being aware of support systems within the community, navigating institutional barriers, and empowering members, as well as advocating for change at various levels in the system, become even more paramount in support groups. Finally, the ongoing processing and reflective practices of group facilitators, as well as appropriate evaluation of the effectiveness of support groups, are necessary best practice components in facilitating support groups.

Support groups are typically perceived as occurring face to face; however, with the increasing use of technology in today's world, new frontiers are being explored in providing online and other technology-based support groups. Some of the issues related to online groups are discussed in the next section.

Technology-Based Support Groups

Support offered through the use of technology such as e-mail, bulletin boards, telephone conferences, chat groups, and newer programs such as Skype and Adobe Connect provides a way to reach an audience of people who may live in remote areas, who are physically unable to travel, and/or who prefer to remain anonymous (Fukkink & Hermans, 2009; Page et al., 2000). Online groups may be asynchronous—such as when conducted via an e-mail listserve, where there is a time delay between responses—or synchronous—such as in a live chat, where members are logged in at the same time and interacting in real time. In both cases, communication is conducted via text, with no auditory or visual cues. This lack of relay of visual and auditory cues, however, may lead to feelings of impersonality, as well as frustration over delays in communication (Page et al., 2000). The use of software programs featuring avatars and other creative visual cues can help alleviate the problems encountered in faceless interactions. Page et al. (2000) describe the use of a software program called *The Palace,* which places the participants in a virtual room with the use of avatars (pictures or cartoon characters that visually represent the participants) and messages that pop up as balloons. Group planning and implementation in such groups have a different set of challenges and require familiarity with and access to the type of technology being used. Additional time and effort is needed to orient the members to the use of the technology. Nonetheless, the Internet is yet another way to offer support.

In a qualitative study examining the perspectives of members in an asynchronous online support group for individuals who self-injure, Haberstroh and Moyer (2012) found that group participants benefited from this type of support, particularly the therapeutic aspect of writing and receiving encouragement from others who were experiencing similar struggles. While the results of this study are not generalizable, the authors offered some insight into the therapeutic aspects of online support, as well as the challenges in trying to access online support. For instance, some message boards on the Internet provide graphic instructions on how to self-injure, thus promoting the behaviors rather than preventing them. Clearly, much more research is needed to study the effectiveness of online and other technology-based support as the demand for such support continues to grow.

Research and Effectiveness in Support and Self-Help Groups

Mental health professionals have noted a mixed client response to self-help groups. While some report benefiting greatly, with a lifetime commitment to the group, others evaluate the experience as negative (Riordan & Beggs, 1987). In reporting a summary of research results, Riordan and Beggs identify various characteristics of well-functioning self-help groups. They include feelings of getting help by helping, risk-taking by group members, willingness to share leadership responsibilities and self-disclosure on the part of leaders, and a creation of a substitute culture. Support groups are sometimes found to be better utilized than actual intervention or remedial programs. A study by Kupprat, Dayton, Guschlbauer, and Halkitis (2009) on utilization of support groups for substance abuse by 4,134 HIV-positive women in New York city indicates that more than 70% of these women used support services, compared with 35% using mental health services and 48% using substance-abuse services. Effectiveness of self-help groups is also well documented. Kyrouz, Humphreys, and Loomis (2002) cite several studies addressing groups related to addiction, mental health, and physical illness that demonstrate the usefulness of self-help mutual aid groups. The use of self-help and support groups may also result in reduced health care costs related to mental health. Reduced hospitalizations and shorter stays are found to be correlated with self-help groups for mental health (Solomon, 2004). Furthermore, participation in support groups provides greater connection to other formal social support systems such as health care providers, professional helpers, agencies, day-care facilities, and early childhood programs (Strozier, 2012). To assess the effectiveness of such a wide range of self-help and support groups creates a challenge; nevertheless, the need remains for continued research using well-designed methodology that compares the effectiveness of support and self-help groups with various other interventions and support systems. An even more important aspect is how to translate research into practice. In a discussion on evidence-based practice in group work in community settings, Pollio and McGowan (2010) remind us that problems with evidence-based practice are twofold: (1) Best practice models developed by researchers don't always translate well in the "real world," and (2) there is no clear evidence of effective pedagogy on how best to teach group workers to conduct evidence-based practice. It is critical, therefore, that we continue to examine not only what makes support and self-help groups (albeit, *all* groups) effective but also how we teach group workers to incorporate best practice methods in conducting effective groups.

Examples of Support Groups

As discussed earlier, support groups may be offered in a variety of settings and for a variety of reasons. Discussed below are examples of two very different types of support groups—one in a residential treatment setting and the other in a community mental health agency setting.

"Kids of Color Group": A Support Group in a Predominantly White Residential Treatment Setting

As a way to provide support to adolescents of color in a predominantly White residential treatment setting for emotionally and behaviorally disturbed children, the first author (Merchant), along with other colleagues, helped implement a psychoeducational group that provided a forum to address cultural and racial issues (see Merchant & Butler, 2002, for a detailed description of the group). This group, which was initially implemented in 1994, continues to be offered 19 years later, with some minor changes in substance and format. The second author (Yozamp) is currently working in this residential setting and has periodically facilitated and or observed the group over the past few years. The name "Kids of Color Group" evolved among the members themselves early in the implementation of the group and, surprisingly, has stuck to the present day. The group fits the description of a *culture-specific* group (Merchant, 2006, 2009), as it pertains to a group of people who share similar experiences due to their cultural background. Outlined below is a description of the group that serves as an example of how the ASGW *Best Practice Guidelines* (Thomas & Pender, 2008) and *Multicultural and Social Justice Competence Principles for Group Workers* (Singh et al., 2012) can be applied in conducting such a support group.

Planning

Determining Need and Partnering With the Target Population. The group grew out of a need expressed by residents and staff of color in response to lack of attention to cultural and racial issues they experienced in the predominantly White setting. As the clinical and diversity consultant to the agency, I (Merchant) was invited to help the agency respond to those needs. Following several discussions held with various residents, staff, and administrators, it was decided that we would form a psychoeducational group that specifically addressed the needs of students of color. This first step is an example of how we partnered with the target population. Staff members of color who played a major role in raising these concerns participated in the designing and facilitating of the group. Getting a "buy-in" from the administration to provide funding and support to offer these groups was also part of this process. The agency subsequently requested that I facilitate the group along with other staff in the agency, which I did for more than 6 years. While a few staff members and administrators were hesitant, fearing "racial segregation," the need for such a group was generally accepted.

Group Purpose. The purpose of the group is to provide an opportunity for ethnic minority residents to establish a positive racial or cultural identity, increase their understanding of their cultural heritage, enhance self-esteem, learn coping and survival skills, and, most important, access a supportive network within a predominantly White treatment setting.

Group Structure. The next stage in planning was determining the nature and structure of the group. We debated whether the group should be open or closed, finally deciding on a semiclosed 8-to-10–week format, where new group members would be invited to join if attrition occurred due to completion of treatment and/or leaving treatment for other reasons. Membership includes both males and females aged 12 to 18, with the size of the group limited to 10 members. The location of the group moved for several years until finally settling in the in-house library. The library is considered a safe and "neutral" setting away from the hubbub of the individual units where the members reside and without exposure to scrutiny and questioning of other residents about the nature of the group. The group is offered in a weekly or biweekly format, depending on the availability of group facilitators and fit with the rest of the treatment-setting schedule. The group time has varied from 1 to 1 1/2 hours over the years. Membership recruitment is based on referrals from unit therapists. A referral form was developed to solicit information on diagnosis, possible behaviors or symptoms that may interfere with group process, readiness to deal with racial and cultural issues, language preferences, acceptance or rejection of their culture, some information on family background (whether adopted, biracial, etc.), living conditions (level of immersion in cultural setting, economic conditions), and cultural and ethnic identity of parents and caregivers. The facilitators hold a screening interview with each of the participants to determine interest and need for such a group. Questions focus on their cultural background, expectations for the group, and experience of being in the minority in the residential setting. A special effort is made to maintain heterogeneity in the group, with a mix of students who are in various stages of accepting their cultural identity and dealing with a range of issues, such as adoption, bicultural identity, and various levels of acculturation to majority society. The heterogeneity allows for members to learn from one another and to serve as a source of motivation for those who are struggling or reluctant.

Selection of Group Facilitators. We initially operated from the assumption that facilitators needed to be counselors of color to gain members' acceptance; however, this assumption was quickly abandoned as we discovered that while the racial and ethnic makeup of group facilitators is important, members responded equally well to White facilitators who are culturally competent. This also addresses the realistic issue that most of the staff is White and availability of facilitators of color is limited. As such, over the years, a cofacilitation model has been adopted, with one ethnic minority individual and another from the majority culture. Cultural and group facilitation competencies are emphasized regardless of the cultural background of the facilitators. At times, we have more than one facilitator, as some of the staff of color express an interest in joining the group as a way to share their own stories and to provide encouragement and support to the adolescent members.

Performing and Processing

Group Norms and Rules. Norms are established early in the group to respect and honor the various cultural traditions and differing voices of group members. Given the nature of the setting and the severity of the emotional and behavioral issues group members experience, rules are established for acceptable behavior in the group. Disruptive or disrespectful behavior is quickly blocked, at times requiring members to leave until they are better able to function in the group.

Group Format and Activities. Originally, the group was offered as a psychoeducational group involving a range of topics. Group activities included sharing stories about cultural background, personal experiences growing up in the family and community (e.g., as a bicultural child, adopted by White parents, or being raised in an impoverished environment), and experiences related to being in the minority. Creative expression was encouraged through such media as poetry, music, song, dance, and artwork. Information was shared on the nature of racism and prejudice, how to navigate difficult situations, and ways to become advocates for change. The group experience usually ended with a celebration that involved food and entertainment. In recent years, the group has become more open-ended and less structured, with greater emphasis on sharing personal stories and offering support to one another. Food is provided at each of the meetings, which is something the members look forward to. Incidentally, an important lesson for us over the years has been that food serves as a major incentive for attendance in any type of group—particularly support groups!

Group Evaluation. We have found that members respond to personal interviews better than to written responses. No formal evaluation has taken place; however, group members over the years have expressed satisfaction with having such a group and consider it an important part of the treatment process—perhaps a reason why it has persisted for 19 years! Institutional support has sometimes wavered, but interest on the part of group facilitators and members has not. Currently, support for this group exists as a line item in the institution budget, thus ensuring the continuation of the group from year to year.

Community Outreach Referral and Education Group: A Support Group for Chemically Dependent Vietnam Veterans

The following sections provide information about a different type of support group held in a small Midwestern town, based on the first author's (Merchant) interview with the group facilitator (Fuchs-Hoeschen, personal communication, November 1, 2011).

Background Information and Purpose of the Support Group

The support group initially grew out of a need for Vietnam veterans who were experiencing difficulties in their marital relationships following the completion of primary chemical dependency treatment. Veterans Affairs initiated the group for male Vietnam veterans who had completed treatment for chemical dependency and had comorbidity with issues related to depression, anxiety, and posttraumatic stress disorder. The local Veterans Affairs hospital provided the services of a trained professional (male social worker) facilitator for the group. The group had met for several months and had bonded well with one another and the facilitator. However, the group was provided a different facilitator (female, inexperienced) whom they did not adjust well to, and soon the hospital decided it would no longer provide the service. The group members on their own sought out another meeting place and facilitator at another mental health agency. Group members experienced minor difficulty transitioning to the new facility, as well as accepting the assigned group facilitator, who was female. Gradually, group members accepted the transition and developed a good working relationship with the facilitator. Although the group's primary purpose was to address family or marital relationships, the underlying issues of chemical dependency were made explicit and the group continued to address both recovery and relationship issues. The group (at the time of the interview) had met for more than 50 weeks.

Format

The group is a closed group comprising 10 White male Vietnam veterans (age range in the 60s) and 5 support persons (spouses and family members). The need for support persons to join the group was identified as a way to directly address relationship issues and enhance the natural support systems of the group members. Eight of the ten members attend the group regularly. The group format is based on the 12-step model; however, not all members identify with Alcoholics Anonymous. The group facilitator is a licensed independent clinical social worker trained in dialectical behavior therapy, with many years of experience in leading groups. She identifies as someone in recovery from substance abuse and strongly believes in the disease model. She uses the Alcoholics Anonymous model as her guiding philosophy in addressing issues, with a specific focus on the 3 Cs of challenging codependency—"You can't control it, you didn't cause it, and you can't cure it." Family members and spouses are "let off the hook" by emphasizing that it was not their fault that their loved ones were chemically dependent.

The group uses a support-group format in that it is not meant to be therapy, although the group may have "therapeutic moments." Group members are encouraged to help one another. The group format is primarily psychoeducational in nature, with a focus on dealing with recovery from substance abuse and interpersonal issues. It is considered different from counseling or psychotherapy in that there is no treatment plan, no diagnostic assessment, and no coordination of care. Each of the veteran members has his own therapist and psychiatric provider.

Group Structure

The group starts with the same reading each week from the books *Twenty-Four Hours a Day* (Anonymous, 1996) and *Courage to Change* (Al-Anon, 2008). The decision to start with this reading was made by the group members themselves. The reading is followed by a check-in based on a topic picked from a "question jar"—an activity developed by the group facilitator. Questions in the jar are based on concepts from the Alcoholics Anonymous *Big Book* and other recovery-based books. The group relies on the facilitator to keep the group on track and address issues as they surface.

Relationships Within and Outside of the Group

The group over time has cycled through various stages, at times not very connected and at other times experiencing much greater connection with one another. Currently, the group is very cohesive, with self-disclosure and level of support both high. Group and family members have relationships outside of the group, getting together for outings and events. All members are invited to these gatherings as a way to avoid forming cliques. Members make it a point to stay connected with all members regardless of the level of involvement in the group.

Conclusion

Self-help or mutual-aid groups and support groups play an important part in the after care or ongoing care of those who are suffering. Mutual-aid and support groups provide comfort and emotional support for "fellow sufferers," as well as a forum for prevention of further distress, a resource for information, and a platform for advocacy. While initially resisted by helping professionals, the exponential growth of self-help and support groups has ultimately resulted in the recognition of their role in the healing process. The advent of new technology and the increased use of the Internet offer yet another way of providing support. Due to their varied yet similar nature, self-help and support groups may be at two ends of the continuum or may overlap considerably in their role and function. Self-help and mutual aid groups such as Alcoholics Anonymous and other 12-step groups have had a significant impact on the development of other groups, such as Parents Anonymous and Emotions Anonymous. What all these groups have in common is a specific ideology and structure in offering support. Support groups, on the other hand, may be smaller groups that emerge as a result of an unmet need in the community, agency, or institution.

Methods of offering support and self-help groups vary considerably; however, the ASGW *Best Practice Guidelines* (Thomas & Pender, 2008) and *Multicultural and Social Justice Competence Principles* (Singh et al., 2012) can serve as guidelines in conducting effective groups. Despite the popularity of self-help and support groups, much needs to be done in the area of conducting research and developing evidence-based practices. Furthermore, the challenge remains in how best to translate research into real-life practice, as well as how to train professionals in using best practices in conducting group work.

Conclusion _____

As limited resources impact communities and the services provided, groups will continue to grow in popularity as a cost-effective means to provide prevention, intervention, and post-intervention treatment. As described in detail throughout the book, effective implementation of groups can be accomplished by following the three Ps delineated in the ASGW *Best Practice Guidelines* (Thomas & Pender, 2008): planning (assessing need and identifying group goals, structure, resources, member screening, and facilitators), performing (generating meaning and therapeutic conditions necessary to maximize the group experience), and processing (the reflective practice of processing group workings with members, supervisors, and colleagues, essential to evaluation and group outcome). Groups are an effective means to bring people together to solve problems, support one another, and accomplish tasks while providing safety and a sense of belonging. The ASGW *Multicultural and Social Justice Competence Principles for Group Workers* (Singh, Merchant, Skudrzyk, & Ingene, 2012) provide a framework for culturally responsive group work application with diverse populations.

What is in store for the future of group work? As the world advances in technology, new problems will continue to emerge, such as cyberbullying and online access to harmful substances or predators. New technology requires a different means of intervention to reach tech-savvy individuals. It may mean that practitioners have a more immediate means to connect with group members outside of the actual group meeting.

Political decisions have a tremendous impact on health care, the military, financial supports, and strategies to help people. If institutions and agencies do not support prevention programs and health insurance does not cover treatment unless it has been diagnosed as a specific disorder, we may be missing opportunities to detect and treat problems before they become life threatening. The decision to send men and women into combat increases the likelihood that they will return with trauma-related issues. This concern will increase the need for services specific to this population. The economy has made it difficult to seek employment, while others have lost jobs. This has increased problems such as substance abuse, depression, and anxiety. Financial restraints have impacted states and counties, limiting their ability to fund services for adults, adolescents, and children with mental health concerns. With the increase in need and the lack of funding, many individuals will go without the assistance they require. Groups are a cost-efficient measure to meet the growing demand for these services.

As stated earlier, groups can sometimes be blurred depending on the type of setting and the approach used by group facilitators or members. Research is difficult, because there is disagreement as to the objective assessment of efficacy. Moreover, there is often a dichotomy between academic theory and clinical practice. Oftentimes, what is learned in the classroom is not practical in an agency setting. These areas of concern provide an opportunity to bridge academics with practice by following the ASGW framework of professional training standards, which define the knowledge, skills, and experiences necessary to do group work. These concepts give rise to the evolution under way to make group work training more consistent with the growing intensity and diversity of demands for group work practice.

As an academic (Merchant) and practitioner (Yozamp) in the field of counseling, we hope that you will appreciate not only the importance of applying academics to group work but also the equal necessity to modify academics based on what works in clinical practice.

Learning Activities ___

Chapter 2: Prevention Groups

1. Think about what prevention groups were offered in your junior high or high school. What kind of prevention group was it, and how did it benefit the participants as well as the school?

2. Explore the timeline of how prevention groups have changed. For instance, what kinds of topics and groups were offered in the 1970s, 1980s, 1990s, and in the past 10 to 15 years? Do you see a change in the type of prevention groups offered over the years?

3. Check out what types of wellness programs are available on your campus and in your community. Are any of those programs group based? If so, what type of group, as defined by the Association for Specialists in Group Work, would it fall under?

4. Research the long-term effectiveness of popular prevention groups— for example D.A.R.E. (Drug Awareness Resource Education), antibullying groups, and so on.

5. Assume that you are going to implement an after-school group for adolescents in a low-income housing complex. What type of group would you set up, and what multicultural and social justice issues are likely to be addressed in such a setting?

Chapter 3: Groups in Remedial Treatment Settings

1. Assume that you are in an inpatient hospital treatment setting for mental health issues and are asked to implement a group for clients who are depressed or have suicidal ideation. What type of group would you set it up as, and what are some key planning, performing, and processing issues you would consider?

2. How would you deal with a group member who is unresponsive to group interventions and process?

3. How would you determine whether the group is effective or not?

4. Identify three types of agencies or settings that offer remedial groups in your community.

Chapter 4: Support and Self-Help Groups

1. What motivating factors might prompt a person to join a support group?

2. As a group facilitator, what therapeutic factors would you want to develop in a support group?

3. Find an open self-help group in your community and attend a session (after obtaining appropriate permission). What type of ideology does that self-help group promote?

4. What types of support groups and self-help groups are offered on your campus and in your community? Are the self-help and support groups described in distinct ways, or are they considered to be one and the same?

References _____

Al-Anon (2008). *Courage to change*. Baltimore, MD: Alanon Family Group Publisher.

Alcoholics Anonymous. (2013). *Estimates of A.A. groups and members as of January 1, 2013*. Retrieved from http://www.aa.org/en_pdfs/smf-53_en.pdf

American heritage dictionary of the English language (4th ed.). (2009). Boston: Houghton Mifflin.

American Self-Help Group Clearinghouse. (2013, July). *Self-help group sourcebook online*. Retrieved from http://mentalhelp.net/selfhelp/

Anonymous. (1996). *Twenty-four hours a day*. Center City, MN: Hazelden.

Blustein, D. L. (1982). Using informal groups in cross-cultural counseling. *Journal for Specialists in Group Work*, 7(4), 260–265.

Bowen, S., Chawla, N., & Marlatt, A. G. (2011). *Mindfulness-based relapse prevention for addictive behaviors: A clinician's guide*. New York: Guilford Press.

Chojnacki, J. T., & Gelberg, S. (1995). The facilitation of a gay/lesbian/bisexual support therapy group by heterosexual counselors. *Journal of Counseling & Development, 73*, 352–354.

Cohen, J. A., Mannarino, A. P., & Deblinger, E. (2006). *Treating trauma and traumatic grief in children and adolescents*. New York: Guilford Press

Conyne, R. K. (1991). Gains in primary prevention: Implications for the counseling profession. *Journal of Counseling and Development, 69*, 277–279.

Conyne, R. K. (2000). Prevention in counseling psychology: At long last, has the time now come? *Counseling Psychologist, 28*, 838–844. doi:10.1177/0011000000 286005

Conyne, R. K. (2003). Best practice in leading prevention groups. *The Group Worker, 32*, 10–13.

Conyne, R. K. (2004). Prevention groups. In J. L. DeLucia-Waack, D. Gerrity, C. Kalodner, & M. Riva (Eds.), *Handbook of group counseling and psychotherapy* (pp. 621–630). Thousand Oaks, CA: Sage.

Conyne, R. K. (2010). *Prevention program development and evaluation: An incidence reduction, culturally relevant approach*. Thousand Oaks, CA: Sage.

Conyne, R. K., & Bemak, F. (2004). Teaching group work from an ecological perspective. *Journal for Specialists in Group Work, 29*, 7–18.

Conyne, R. K., & Horne, A. (2001). The current status of groups being used for prevention. *Journal for Specialists in Group Work, 26*, 289–292.

Conyne, R. K., & Wilson, F. R. (1999). *Psychoeducation group training program* [Video]. New York: Insight Media.

Conyne, R. K., & Wilson, F. R. (2000). Division 49 position paper: Recommendations of the task group for the use of groups for prevention. *Group Psychologist, 11*, 10–11.

Delucia-Waack, J. L. (1997). What do we need to know about group work a cull for future research and theory. *Journal for Specialists in Group Work, 22*(3), 146–148.

DeLucia-Waack, J. L., Gerrity, D. A., Kalodner, C. R., & Riva, M. T. (Eds.). (2004). *Handbook of group counseling and psychotherapy*. Thousand Oaks, CA: Sage.

Elliott, T. R., Rivera, P., & Tucker, E. (2004). Groups in behavioral health and medical settings. In J. L. Delucia-Waack, D. A. Gerrity, C. R. Kalodner, & M. T. Riva (Eds.), *Handbook of group counseling and psychotherapy* (pp. 338–350). Thousand Oaks, CA: Sage.

Emer, D. (2004). The use of groups in inpatient facilities: Needs, focus, successes, and remaining dilemmas. In J. L. Delucia-Waack, D. A. Gerrity, C. R. Kalodner, & M. T. Riva (Eds.), *Handbook of group counseling and psychotherapy*. Thousand Oaks, CA: Sage.

Encyclopedia of Mental Disorders. (2013). Support groups. Retrieved from http://www.minddisorders.com/Py-Z/Support-groups.html

Foy, D. W., Eriksson, C. B., & Trice, G. A. (2001). Introduction to group interventions for trauma survivors. *Group Dynamics: Theory, Research, and Practice, 5*(4), 246–251. doi:10.1037/1089-2699.5.4.246

Fredrickson, B. (2009). *Positivity*. New York: Crown.

Frew, J. E. (1986). Leadership approaches to achieve maximum therapeutic potential in mutual support groups. *Journal for Specialists in Group Work, 11*(2), 93–99.

Fukkink, R. G., & Hermans, J. M. (2009). Children's experiences with chat support and telephone support. *Journal of Child Psychology and Psychiatry, 50*, 759–766. doi:10.1111/j.1469-7610.2008.02024.x

Gallagher-Thompson, D., Arean, P., Rivera, P., & Thompson, L. W. (2001). A psychoeducational intervention to reduce distress in Hispanic family caregivers. *Clinical Gerontologist, 23*, 17–32. doi:10.1300/J018v23n01_03

Gazda, G., & Pistole, C. (1985). Life skills training: A model. *Counseling and Human Development, 19*, 1–7.

Gladding, S. T. (2011). *Groups: A counseling specialty* (6th ed.). Upper Saddle River, NJ: Pearson Education.

Greif, G. L., & Ephross, P. H. (Eds.). (2005). *Group work with populations at risk*. New York: Oxford Press.

Haberstroh, S., & Moyer, M. (2012). Exploring an online self-injury support group: Perspectives from group members. *Journal for Specialists in Group Work, 37*(2), 113–132.

Hage, S., & Romano, J. (2010). History of prevention and prevention groups: Legacy for the 21st century. *Group Dynamics: Theory, Research and Practice, 14*, 199–210.

Harpine, E. C., Nitza, A., & Conyne, R. (2010). Prevention groups: Today and tomorrow. *Group Dynamics: Theory, Research and Practice, 10*(3), 268–280.

Higginbotham, H. N., West, S. G., & Forsyth, D. R. (1988). *Psychotherapy and behavior change: Social, cultural, and methodological perspectives*. New York: Pergamon Press.

Kabat-Zinn, J. (1990). *Full catastrophe living: Using the wisdom of your body and mind to face stress, pain and illness*. New York: Dell.

Kupprat, S. A., Dayton, A. B., Guschlbauer, A., & Halkitis, P. (2009). Case manager-reported utilization of support group, substance use and mental health services among HIV-positive women in New York City. *AIDS Care, 21*(7), 874–880.

Kurtz, L. F. (1997). *Self-help and support groups: A handbook for practitioners.* Thousand Oaks, CA: Sage.

Kyrouz, E. M., Humphreys, K., & Loomis, C. (2002). A review of research on the effectiveness of self-help mutual aid groups. In B. White & E. J. Madara (Eds.), *Self-help group sourcebook* (7th ed., pp. 1–16). Denville, NJ: Saint Clares Health Services.

Merchant, N. M. (2006). Multicultural and diversity competent group work. In J. Trotzer (Ed.), *The counselor and the group* (4th ed., pp. 319–349). Philadelphia: Accelerated Development.

Merchant, N. M. (2009). Types of diversity-related groups. In C. Salazar (Ed.), *Group work experts share their favorite multicultural activity: A guide to diversity-competent choosing, planning, conducting and processing* (pp. 13–24). Alexandria, VA: Association for Specialists in Group Work.

Merchant, N. M., & Butler, M. (2002). Psychoeducational group for ethnic-minority adolescents in a predominantly White treatment setting. *Journal for Specialists in Group Work, 27*(3), 314–332.

National Alliance on Mental Illness. (2012). About NAMI. Retrieved from http://www.nami.org/template.cfm?section=About_NAMI

Owens, P. C., & Kulic, K. R. (2001). What's needed now: Using groups for prevention. *Journal for Specialists in Group Work, 26,* 205–210. doi:10.1080/01933920 108414211

Page, B. J., Delmonico, D. L., Walsh, J., L'amoreaux, N. A., Danninhirsh, C., Thompson, R. S., et al. (2000). Setting up on-line support groups using the Palace software. *Journal for Specialists in Group Work, 25*(2), 133–145.

Parents Anonymous. (2012). Vision, mission and history. Retrieved from http://parentsanonymous.org/about-us/mission-history/

Pearson, R. E. (1983). Support groups: A conceptualization. *Personnel and Guidance Journal, 61,* 361–364. doi:10.1111/j.2164-4918.1983.tb00044.x

Pollio, D. E., & Macgowan, M. J. (2010). From the guest editors: Introduction to evidence-based group work in community settings. *Social Work with Groups, 33,* 98–101.

Recovery International. (2013). History of Recovery International. Retrieved from http://www.lowselfhelpsystems.org/about/history.asp

Riordan, R., & Beggs, M. (1987). Counselors and self-help groups. *Journal of Counseling and Development, 65,* 427–429.

Romano, J. L., & Hage, S. M. (2000). Prevention and counseling psychology: Revitalizing commitments for the 21st century. *Counseling Psychologist, 28,* 733–763. doi:10.1177/0011000000286001

Schopler, J. H., & Galinsky, M. J. (1995). Expanding our view of support groups as open systems. *Social Work with Groups, 18*(1), 3–10.

Silverman, P. (2002). Understanding self-help groups. In B. White & E. J. Madara (Eds.), *The self-help group sourcebook: Your guide to community and online support groups* (7th ed., pp. 25–38). Denville, NJ: Saint Clares Health Services.

Singh, A., Merchant, N., Skudrzyk, B., & Ingene, D. (2012). Association for Specialists in Group Work: Multicultural and social justice competence principles for group workers. *Journal for Specialists in Group Work, 37*(4), 277–296.

Smith, K. (2012, April 29). 5 prevention programs GOP hopes to target. *Politico*. Retrieved from http://www.politico.com/news/stories/0412/75723.html

Society for Prevention Research. (2009). A call for bold action to support prevention programs and policies. Retrieved from https://docs.google.com/viewer?url= http%3A%2F%2Fwww.preventionresearch.org%2FSPR_T2_Task_Force_ Position_Statement.pdf

Solomon, P. (2004). Peer support/peer provided services underlying processes, benefits, and critical ingredients. *Psychiatric Rehabilitation Journal, 27*(4), 392–401.

Strozier, A. L. (2012). The effectiveness of support groups in increasing social support for kinship caregivers. *Children and Youth Services Review, 34*(5), 876–888.

Subrahmanyan, L., & Merchant, N. (2006). Cultural identity psychoeducational groups: A multidisciplinary, multi-aged, and multi-institutional approach. *Group Worker, 35*(1).

Thomas, R. V., & Pender, D. A. (2008). Association for Specialists in Group Work: Best practice guidelines 2007 revisions. *Journal for Specialists in Group Work, 33*, 111–117. doi:10.1080/01933920801971184

Waldo, M., & Bauman, S. (1998). Regrouping the categorization of group work: A goals and process (GAP) matrix for groups. *Journal for Specialists in Group Work, 23*, 164–176.

Wilson, F. R., Rapin, L. S., & Haley-Banez, L. (2000). *Professional standards for the training of group workers*. Retrieved from http://asgw.org/pdf/training_ standards.pdf

Yalom, I. D. (1983). *Inpatient group psychotherapy*. New York: Basic Books.

Yalom, I. D. (with Leszcz, M.). (2005). *Theory and practice of group psychotherapy* (5th ed.). New York: Basic Books.

Index_____

About the Authors _____

Niloufer M. Merchant, EdD, LP, NCC, has been a professor in the Community Psychology undergraduate and Community Counseling graduate programs at St. Cloud State University (SCSU) since 1991. She is an active member of the American Counseling Association (ACA) and Association for Specialists in Group Work (ASGW), a division of ACA. She served as president of ASGW in 2011–2012. She has held other leadership positions, including department chair (2004–2010), board president for the Multicultural Center of Central Minnesota (2005–2007), interim director of the SCSU Women's Center (2002–2003), and interim cultural diversity director for St. Cloud School District (1999–2000). Merchant is a licensed psychologist and national certified counselor, providing clinical and consulting services in the community. She also provides in-services and trainings in the area of cultural competence. Her scholarship and interest areas include group work, multicultural counseling and competence, women's issues, mindfulness-based practices, and social justice issues. She is coauthor of the *ASGW Multicultural and Social Justice Competence Principles for Group Workers* (2012).

Carole J. Yozamp, MS, LPC, was employed as a clinical manager/therapist in residential treatment at the St. Cloud Children's Home in St. Cloud, Minnesota, starting in 2005. Recently, Yozamp accepted a new position as staff psychotherapist at a partial mental health hospitalization program for adolescents. Carole is a licensed professional counselor with a master of science in community psychology and criminal justice. She has an extensive work history with the University of Minnesota Extension Service and the Minnesota Department of Corrections. She is a skilled individual, family, and group facilitator.